# TORTURED BLUES

ISBN–13: 978-1-937458-96-6

Printed in the United States of America.

This publication is designed to provide entertainment value and is sold with the understanding that the publisher is not engaged in rendering legal, accounting, or other professional advice of any kind. If legal advice or other expert assistance is required, the services of a competent professional person should be sought.

—From a Declaration of Principles jointly adopted by a Committee of the American Bar Association and a Committee of Publishers and Associations

# TORTURED BLUES

BLAIR REDD

# DEDICATION

To Ty,
You always followed your dreams, giving
me the courage to follow mine.

To Roseann,
I know you put up with a lot, but this
dream could not have been a reality
without your support.

# CONTENTS

# CHAPTER 1

Nolan trembled. His black-and-blue eyes were on the brink of being completely swelled shut, and his throat bled raw as he screamed for help. Trying to keep his sanity, he recounted over and over what the police academy had trained him to do if he ever became a hostage. The concrete walls were the perfect place for torture. Nolan shivered as the water continued to drip onto his head. His shirt was soaked, and he wished he could rip it off for any little bit of warmth. The fibers from the rope were cutting off all feeling to his hands and ankles. His chin slouched down to his chest. Even if he could escape, it would be like running in quicksand. The only thought that kept him from complete lunacy was the idea of reuniting with his mom. Breaking up a drug ring was the only thing Nolan wanted as a cop; and now his unquenchable desire for that may have cost him his life.

Two men walked into the room. One of them had a cheap, red tracksuit on. He was a small man with skinny legs. He slicked his brown hair back as if he had just gotten out of the shower. He had a scar on his left cheek as if he'd been cut. The other man followed him like a lost puppy. He had dirty-blonde hair and a big, burly beard, and he was a well-built, powerful man. Without saying a word, they grabbed a wet nylon sack, placed it over Nolan's head, and cut off the ropes that were binding him. Nolan tried to throw a punch, but he couldn't lift his arms. He struggled as they placed his head at the bottom of a slanted board. He heard the big guy speak in a thick Southern accent. "Are you sure we should be doing this? He's just a kid."

In an eerily calm voice, the smaller man, with an English accent, said, "He's a cop. That's all I need to know about him."

The two men grabbed a bucket full of water and slid it down the board. Nolan fought for air, but he swallowed way too much. Water started to fill up his lungs. With his last ounce of adrenaline, he flailed his arms and legs wildly, but the powerful man picked him up and slammed him down. He felt his forearm in his back, and he couldn't move. The water stopped coming, and they removed the sack from his head, but he still felt like he was in the ocean. As he closed his eyes, he wondered if he was ever going to open them again.

Nolan felt a hard shot to his face. He opened his eyes to see the man with the calm voice looking at him with a sheepish grin. Nolan didn't know if he was in hell or back in the cold dark room. Sharp pains shot through his entire body. He couldn't talk, only mumble. His stomach was twisting inside out. He knew he was going to die, but he didn't know how long it would take for his body to give out.

"So, cop," the man from England said. "Sneaking around my warehouse is a good way to get yourself killed."

Nolan looked up and pleaded with his eyes to let him go. The man continued to speak. "I want to know what you are doing here. It's really a very simple question." Nolan realized the man wasn't going to let him go. Nolan gathered all his strength and motioned for the man to come closer. As the man leaned in, Nolan spit in his face. He wiped the spit from his face, grabbed a broomstick, and broke it over Nolan's head.

"You have some guts, son. Too bad they're all going to be spilled over my floor in a couple of seconds."

The man motioned for the other one to come over. Nolan couldn't understand why such a massive man was taking orders from a puny Crumpet-Stuffer. He brought his boss a .45-caliber hand gun. Nolan closed his eyes and prayed that the bullet wouldn't be too excruciating. Nolan felt the cold steel press against his temple and heard the cock of the gun. He heard the loud crack of a gun, but he didn't feel anything. Nolan wondered if he was dead. He opened his eyes and, to his amazement, saw the man in the red suit on the ground clutching his chest. He pulled his hands away from his chest and looked at them. They were covered in blood and he gargled. His body went limp and he was dead. Nolan looked bewildered at the other man.

"Don't crap your pants, kid. I'm on the job," he said with his thick Southern accent. He pulled his badge out of his leather jacket. He continued, "What kind of a cop comes snooping around a known mobster's warehouse without any backup while wearing a police uniform?"

"I didn't know whose warehouse this was," Nolan mumbled. "I was checking out a disturbance call at this address."

The undercover cop called an ambulance for both Nolan and the mobster he just shot. "Kid, I have a lot of time invested into finding out where this nutjob hid all of his bodies, and I don't have any of that information."

The undercover looked Nolan in the eye. Nolan didn't know whether the concern on the undercover's face was about his health or the case that just blew up, but it was there. "It's not the end of the world; I personally witnessed him trying to kill a cop. That will get him twenty-five to life, and now I can sleep in my own bed tonight."

The ambulance arrived and treated Nolan. The EMT gave him some painkillers, and he felt his eyes get very heavy.

When he opened his eyes, he saw his grandpa sitting there along with the police chief in his hospital room. By the bags under his grandpa's eyes, he could tell that he hadn't slept for at least two days. The chief, also known as Lou, had his head in his hands. Nolan glanced at them and finally broke the silence, "Water."

His grandpa sprinted towards the water fountain. He poured a big glass full of cold water and handed it to Nolan. As he took the glass from his grandpa, he recalled the man with the calm voice and the water filling up his lungs. He put it down, and he started to shake. His Grandpa grabbed Nolan and reassured him he wasn't in any more harm.

"Not thirsty?" his Grandpa said. He turned towards Lou and grabbed the Coke out of his hand. "Here, son, drink this." Nolan took the soda from his grandpa and gulped it down.

Nolan sat up and asked, "Lou, what happened to the man who tortured me?"

Lou was dressed in his blues. He was always dressed in them. He stood up, and his head almost touched the ceiling. It was a small room, but Lou was a giant of a man. Lou gave a couple of chuckles, then a confused look crept over his face. "Are you serious, Nolan?"

"Yes, I am. I want to know."

"He was killed by the FBI. You were sitting right there. An undercover agent saved your life."

"Who was that undercover who saved my life?"

"Don't really know much about him. I guess he's from the Salt Lake City FBI. He wants to slap you in the face for screwing up his case. He also wants to shake your hand for the bravery you displayed. He didn't know which one he would do first, though."

Nolan didn't think he was brave. In fact, he thought of himself as incompetent for getting caught and a coward for screaming when he was bound. The undercover agent who infiltrated an English mafia family was the type of brave Nolan wanted to be. He leaned over towards Lou. "I want to go undercover."

Nolan's grandpa jumped up with anger. "You aren't even close to being ready. I spent forty-three years on the force, and not once did I get captured and tortured."

"I have to agree with Jared, Nolan. It takes years to gain the skills to work undercover, and I don't think you're there," Lou said.

Nolan wasn't going to take no for an answer. "Grandpa, I know you were a great cop, but I just withstood endless torture, and even the man from Salt Lake thinks I have the stones." He turned and pleaded with Lou. "I can do it; I'm only twenty-three, but I'm the fastest-rising officer in the force."

Lou whispered something to Nolan's grandpa. The two of them go way back. Lou was the only person that his Grandpa allowed to call him by his God-given name of Jared.

"Nolan," Lou said, "I got something starting in August. If you agree to live with your grandpa, Jared, it's yours."

"Really?" Nolan stood up with excitement. His body, still under excruciating pain, collapsed right back onto the bed.

"Here's the catch," Lou said. "Your grandpa is going to be your point person on this. What he says goes. It's a high school assignment. The principal is a friend of mine, and he's the only person who will know who you are once you get there."

"Yes, sir. Of course."

With that, Lou shook Nolan's hand and exited the room. Nolan's grandpa's eyes watered, and he gave Nolan a big hug. "I don't like it, but if this is what you feel like you need to do, then I'm not going to stand in your way."

For the rest of the night, Nolan laid back in his bed, his mind running wild envisioning all of the cases he was going to bust wide open and all of the accolades that were sure to come his way. There wasn't anything stopping him now.

# CHAPTER 2

*P*icking the right shirt on the first day of school
had more of an impact on making friends than
just about anything else that Nolan could do. On his
first day of his sophomore year, he spent three days
combing through his attire determining what would
make him stick out. It had been a long time since he
had to start a new school, and Nolan's stomach was
filled with butterflies. There wasn't any time to prepare
for the school year, and the amount of pressure to fit in
weighed on him like an anchor. It's not that he wanted
to look nice; after all, his shaggy, dirty blonde hair, tan
complexion, and athletic physique already managed to
get him into enough trouble the first go-around of high
school. He knew what crowd he needed to run with, and
his polo shirts and khaki pants just weren't going to do
him any favors.

"Jared, I need to wear your shirt that has the eagle on it," Nolan yelled.

"I filled your closet with shirts just before you got here. By the way, the name's Grandpa to you."

"They all shout eighteen-year-old virgin."

"I wanted your shirts to match your personality."

"Oh, you're splitting my sides, Grandpa. Can I wear the shirt or not?"

"I've never met a cop who's so panicked about what teenagers were going to think of him. Of course, you're twenty-three years old and live with your grandpa, so you may have a reason to be edgy."

Jared tossed him the shirt and gave him a wry smile. Jared had a rough edge around him but had the biggest heart of anyone Nolan knew. He retired from the police force five years prior, but when the assignment required Nolan to stay in his house, Jared felt the rush of being back on the force. Not many people get to end on a high note from their career. This was Jared's chance to put a fairytale ending on his career. The hard part of this assignment was to get Nolan to buy into his strategies.

"Alright, Grandpa, I'm heading out."

"Nolan, come here for a minute."

Nolan approached his grandfather and sat down beside him. Jared's face was stoic. Nolan was all ears as Jared agonized over the words that he wanted Nolan to hear.

"I know you've been a cop for three years, but this is the first time you've been on your own. These kids you meet, some are going to be nice, some are going to have fancy toys, and some are going to be quiet. It's your job to sort out who's who. It's not time to have fun and make new friends. It's time to do your job. You have to be a damn good actor to go undercover."

"Grandpa, you think I don't know what I'm doing?"

"I never said that. That's the problem I'm trying to explain to you. You have to listen. Listen to what's going on everywhere, listen to what the girl who sits alone at the lunch table has to say, listen to what the hip teacher has to say, listen to absolutely anything and everything. So far in life, you're a horrendous listener. That needs to change the moment you step onto campus. Everyone thinks going undercover is about action. If you take action before you're sure action needs to be taken, you're going to end up fired, in jail, or dead. You need to have them come to you. You can't go and introduce yourself as the new kid and ask them to sell you stolen merchandise, drugs, or their soul. Make them want to come to you. Make them feel like they need you more than you need them. That's when you'll have them."

"Thanks, Grandpa, for the advice; but I do things my way. That's why Lou assigned me," Nolan said.

Jared clutched Nolan by both shoulders. "He assigned you because you're the only one on the force who can't grow a beard."

Nolan pulled away and ran out the door. He jumped into his white Honda Accord and waved to his grandpa. With his grandpa's advice falling on deaf ears, Nolan drove to Red Rock High School. The short drive to the school had some beautiful landscape. St. George had some of the most unique mountains in America. The high school got its name from the red mountain ranges all over the valley. Only in Southern Utah could you find palm trees and mountain ranges. It's one of the hidden wonders, as far as Nolan was concerned.

Nolan found a parking spot close to the main doors. He noticed a burly man shooting darts at him with his piercing eyes. The man's baggy basketball shorts, a long sleeve Nike shirt, and muscular shoulders, yet large stomach, were a dead giveaway to Nolan that this was the physical education teacher.

"Teachers' lot. Move your piece of junk," he said.

"I didn't know. It's my first day, and it's not like there are any signs saying this is a teachers' lot."

"Just move the damn thing."

Nolan nodded his head and got back into the car. He found a space on the road about half a mile away from the school. Because of the parking spot he got, he was running late to the meeting he had with Lawrence Bitton, the school's principal. As far as Nolan knew, Bitton was the only person on the entire campus that knew he would be coming to Red Rock. Nolan had met with Bitton once before and didn't come away impressed by this aging, overweight, balding excuse for a man. He rambled on about his dogs when Nolan asked him what the biggest concern at Red Rock High was. Bitton was as sharp as a marble, and that's the main reason that Nolan has to spend the next few months back in the hell that is otherwise known as high school.

Nolan knocked on the door and crept in before being invited. "What's going on, Lawrence?" Nolan said casually.

"Oh Nolan. It's so good to see you. Did I tell you about how my wife makes the best apple pie you've ever tasted?"

"Yes, you have. Is that how you start every conversation? I'm starting to see a trend."

Bitton laughed, "That's a good one, Nolan. Seriously, though, her trick is the grapes. Nobody ever puts grapes in the apple pie."

"Uh-huh. Grapes you say. Where's my class schedule?"

"Ah yes, your schedule. Let me retrieve that for you."

"Hey, Lawrence," Nolan began his probe. "There was a gym teacher, balding dark hair, olive skin, broad shoulders, and he was giving me the business about parking in the teachers' lot."

"Oh, you must've met Rocco Porter. He's from Texas and isn't very happy about teaching and coaching in Utah. Back in Texas I guess he won a lot of football games, but an incident with one of his players got blown out of proportion, and he was fired. Their loss is our gain. He's brought our football team back from the grave."

"So he's a coach. That explains his death stare."

"If he only looked your way, consider yourself lucky. If you don't want to draw any attention to yourself, you need to stay under his radar. Don't park in the teachers' lot, don't mouth off to him, don't piss him off is all I'm saying."

"Thanks for the tip, I guess," Nolan said as he rolled his eyes at Bitton.

Nolan yanked his schedule from Bitton and walked out of his office. *The principal is scared of the football coach. I can see why this school is in trouble*, Nolan thought. Nolan looked down at his schedule and noticed Spanish 3 was his first class. He didn't know what he was going to do in a Spanish class. Nolan never spoke a word of it in his life. Nolan saw room 335, opened the door, took a deep breath, and slipped into class.

Opening a classroom door after the bell has rung isn't the best way to keep a low profile. A stunning blonde-haired, green-eyed Spanish teacher in a tight, red skirt spoke to him. "Hola, joven. ¿Qué estás haciendo en mi clase?"

She was so beautiful that he would've been too mesmerized to understand what she said even if it were in English. He had no chance of understanding what she said in Spanish.

"I don't know what you just said," Nolan said as his face turned red.

"What are you doing in my class?" She strode over to him, one leg in front of the other.

"I don't know. The fat man pointed me in this direction. I'm new to this school."

"Well if you couldn't understand what I just said, you obviously don't belong in this class."

"I couldn't agree more. However, here I am, and this is what my schedule says, so I don't know what else to do. If you have a suggestion, I'm more than open to hear you out."

"Take a seat and get it fixed at lunch."

"Sounds like a plan."

"Sit down."

Nolan scanned the classroom and saw an empty seat in the middle of the room. He hurried to the desk and sat down. Nolan wanted to come across as a tough guy, but this was going to be more difficult than Nolan anticipated. He was used to being a class clown, and he didn't want to fall back into that as soon as he was put into an uncomfortable situation.

About an hour later, Nolan heard the bell ring. It was the first thing that he understood since he sat down. Nolan glanced at his schedule to see where this misery train's next stop was. *AP English. What in the world was going through Bitton's mind?* Nolan thought. *Spanish 3 and AP English as the first two classes?* Nolan stormed into Bitton's office and slammed the door.

"Lawrence, what kind of schedule is this? I don't speak Spanish, and if I wanted to take college courses, I would've stayed in college."

"Forgive me, Nolan. It's not that easy to put a schedule together in a week's time. I'm not sure what's even going on here?"

"We can agree on that," Nolan said.

"I assumed you wouldn't even be attending the classes. I thought you would be out with the parking lot crew. Isn't that where all the action's at?"

"I have my ways, Lawrence. I won't tell you you should eat better, and you won't tell me how to bust drug dealers."

"Okay, Nolan," Bitton said exasperated. "Go give this note to Mr. Erickson. His office is 112. He's the guidance counselor. He should be able to fix your schedule."

Nolan took the note from Bitton and read it.

"Jim, please make a new schedule for Nolan Graham. I just received his transcripts, and he's not nearly smart enough for his current schedule. Thanks, Lawrence."

"That jerk," Nolan whispered. Nolan went up and down the hallways searching for Mr. Erickson's office. He wandered around the halls trying to deduce how the number system in the school worked. Nolan couldn't find ice in the arctic, so trying to find an office in a three story school was close to impossible for him.

Nolan heard a deep gruff voice, "Hey kid, do you know what you're doing?"

Nolan spun around and looked at a man who was too young to be a teacher, but too old to be a student. He stood well over six feet tall with a shaved head and a grizzly beard. His T-shirt was two sizes too small, but Nolan figured it was to show off his biceps and chest, which were chiseled like a Greek god.

"No, not really; it's my first day," Nolan said.

"I've seen you pass through the hall three times. Where are you heading?"

Nolan felt the hot rush of embarrassment overcoming him, so he fired back the only way he knew how to, "Are you some kind of hall monitor? I'm sure your parents must be proud."

The young man stuck his hands in his jean pockets and smirked at Nolan, "I'm not the one who's been strolling through the halls inspecting every door number. From my viewpoint, it looks like you're the one monitoring the halls."

Nolan gave a faux smile; after all, he could appreciate a good ribbing. "Yeah, I guess I am. I'm Nolan, the new kid. Principal Bitton gave me this note to give to Mr. Erickson, but I can't seem to find his office."

"I've got good news for you. You're two doors down from Mr. Erickson's office. Room 244."

"244? Bitton said it was room 112."

"That's funny. We don't have rooms in the one hundreds. Either Lawrence is losing his mind or you did something to get under his skin. I'm guessing the latter. Lawrence is very clever."

"Clever? Lawrence Bitton? Are you sure we're talking about the same guy? He talks about grapes in apple pies?" Nolan said in a high-pitched voice.

"If you don't think he's clever, then you've already lost the battle with him. Lawrence didn't become the principal because he's dumb."

"There is no way that I lost a battle of wits to Lawrence Bitton. It's just not possible," Nolan said.

"I can't say if you did or you didn't. All I know is that he's sitting in his office, and you're walking the halls looking for a room that doesn't exist."

"Fair enough, Hall Monitor."

"As much as I like being called Hall Monitor, my friends call me Ken." Ken turned the corner, and just like that, Nolan went back to looking for the guidance counselor's office.

Nolan didn't know if Ken was having a little fun at his expense or if he was genuine about Bitton being clever . . . not that it mattered to Nolan. He was there for one reason; and a high school principal, who may or may not be clever, wasn't going to stand in his way.

# CHAPTER 3

*J*uice knew he was the man at Red Rock High School. The faculty may have been the figureheads of the school, but everyone knew that Juice ran the place. There wasn't anyone who came in or out of the school who didn't get introduced to Juice. How could you miss him? He was the resident bodybuilder, and he even started a weightlifting club at the school. This was his way of sticking it to Coach Rocco Porter. If he could get a few of the football players in his lifting crew, he could talk them out of playing football.

Juice had been the best player on the football team, but Coach Porter threw him off the team for knocking one of the assistant coaches out cold with one punch. Juice tried to apologize to both coaches, but they weren't having anything to do with it. That surprised him a little bit since he and the assistant coach, Ken, had been good friends. Ken was only a couple years older than Juice, and their families lived across the street on Buena Vista Drive growing up. The toughest part of not being on the team for Juice was that Karen, his ex-girlfriend, was also Coach Porter's daughter. Since her mother left them, she always took her father's side in an argument . . . no matter what. Coach Porter never liked the two of them dating. A redneck from Texas hated a black man dating his daughter. Sure, they were good enough to run routes, block, and tackle for him, but one dating his daughter was unacceptable. When Juice punched the assistant coach, it had to feel like Coach Porter won the lottery. He kicked him off the team and out of his daughter's life.

Juice's temper had gotten him into more trouble than just getting kicked off a football team. He was in deep to some people who made him break out in cold sweats at night. Half the reason he snapped on the coaches had to do with the life he led outside the football field.

Juice wasn't so much of a student at Red Rock, but a figurehead. He looked at going to class as his payment for a gym membership. If all he had to do was sit through a few classes a day to get free use of the weight room, well that was more than worth it. He trained to be a professional bodybuilder, so he figured he didn't need to pay attention to Utah history. That wasn't going to get him closer to his dreams. He wanted to skip high school altogether, but he made a bet with his mom that he could finish it. The competitive nature in Juice wasn't going to allow him to lose a bet.

He opened the door to the weight room and saw Karen working out. Even after they broke up, Juice still couldn't help but be astonished by her looks. Juice walked up behind her and trapped her by the curl station. "What's up, girl?"

Karen tried to maneuver around him, but Juice kept blocking her path. "Juice, leave me alone. I'm trying to finish my workout before school starts."

Juice stepped away from her, "Excuse me, princess. We can't have you late for class. It's not like your daddy won't write you a note."

Karen picked up a twenty-pound barbell and started curling it. She finished her set and got really close to Juice. She stood on her tiptoes to reach him and whispered, "I could get a note from my dad like we used to when we would fool around before school in his office."

Juice rubbed his hands together, raised his eyebrows, and got a huge schoolboy grin on his face. "Yeah girl, exactly like that."

Karen turned around and grabbed her weight again. "I work out longer than two minutes now."

Juice grabbed Karen by the hair, spun her around, and pointed his finger in her face. "Don't you ever disrespect me. I don't care if you're a man or a woman. I will cave your skull in."

He let her go and walked back out into the hallway. He bumped into the first person he could see in the halls . . . a small sophomore who Juice didn't know. "Do you got a problem, son?"

The sophomore turned away and went into a full sprint. Juice started his cocky walk. Still got this.

# CHAPTER 4

Nolan left his schedule in Mr. Erickson's office and headed out into the halls. Mr. Erickson told him to finish out the school day with his old schedule and he could start fresh the next day. Nolan didn't want to go to classes that he wasn't going to keep, so he decided to do a little snooping around. The kids who didn't go to class and hung out in the halls were the ones he wanted to get to know anyway. The idea may have been put into his head by Bitton, but Nolan's ego let him believe that he came up with this plan all by himself. When he was wandering the halls looking for Mr. Erickson's office, he saw a few students talking in a small room. Nolan thought he would start there and see what these students were up to.

Nolan rounded the hallway corner and saw the door closed to where the kids were. He tried looking through the window in the door, but the dirt and dust accumulated from thirty years of nobody cleaning it obscured his view. Nolan could hear voices in the room, so he knocked on the door to see if anyone would answer. The door swung open so fast that Nolan had to jump back to avoid getting hit. Standing in the doorway appeared the most stunningly gorgeous, olive-skinned, dark-haired goddess Nolan had ever laid eyes on. Her hair was pulled back in a ponytail, and her shorts were cut well above the knee.

"Can I help you?"

Nolan, not knowing what to say, mumbled, "Uh, hi. What are you doing in there?"

The girl peering at Nolan cautiously said, "We're in the middle of class. What are you doing?"

Nolan browsed the room and counted the kids, "What type of class only has five kids in it?"

"Student Body Officer prep class. That's kind of the only reason that anybody runs for SBO officer. We get a free class period to do what we want."

Nolan knew at this point that these weren't the kids that he needed to be investigating, but her smile made the sun seem dim, and he didn't want to leave just yet. Nolan didn't meet stunning girls walking the beat, so he tried to flirt with her, "You're an SBO, huh?"

"I am. This is actually my second time being an officer."

Nolan crept closer to the door trying to get inside. "I thought only seniors could be SBO officers?"

"Yep."

"I'm confused." Nolan said

She stepped to the side a little giving Nolan a little bit of hope that he could come in. "What class are you cutting?"

"Uh, well, you see, my schedule isn't ready until tomorrow, so I don't really have anywhere to go."

She turned her back to Nolan leaving the door open. "I don't care if you come in here, but keep your mouth shut while I run through our events."

Nolan hurried in and saw that this wasn't a classroom but an entertainment center. Couches, beanbags, television, and video game consoles . . . these kids had a sanctuary for two hours a day. Nolan took a seat on one of the beanbags. He stayed out of the way while they talked about Homecoming week. Bonfires, pep-rallies, Red Rock lovin', as far as Nolan could tell, were all just reasons for the senior class to go out on the football field and make out with each other. After the officers had finished talking about the Homecoming, the only boy in the room turned on a football video game.

"Hey bro, you want to play me?"

"Sure," Nolan said. "Prepare for a loss." Nolan had one vice in his life, and that was video games.

The boy tossed him a paddle. "So what's the deal with your president? Why has she been an officer twice?" Nolan asked

"Karen? She transferred from out of state where she was an officer for the first month of her senior year. I guess her credits didn't match up or something like that. Instead of being a senior when she got here, her credits only equaled enough to make her a junior."

"Wait, so she's a year older than you guys?"

"Maybe you'll have to be held back a year. I'm pretty sure I just said she was held back a year, so that would make her a year older," the boy said.

Nolan looked at him annoyed. "Fair enough."

As Nolan sat back and relaxed for the first time since he arrived at Red Rock, one of the girls asked in a curious manner, "You're telling me that on your first day at a new school, they didn't have your schedule ready?"

Nolan's eyes shifted towards her, "They had a schedule ready, but it wasn't the right one. Mr. Erickson is taking care of it today."

"Schedule too hard for you?"

"Christy, be quiet." Karen came to Nolan's defense. "For all we know, it could've been too easy."

"No," Christy said condescendingly, "he was in my first period Spanish class. Trust me, he knows next to nothing about Spanish."

Nolan chimed in quickly, "Yeah, not everyone can have a class as hard as sitting on a couch drinking a flavor-of-the-month vitamin drink . . . like you."

"Stop it," Karen said to Nolan. "If you want to stay in this room, stop with the second grade insults. You too, Christy."

"Whatever," Christy said as she rolled her eyes at Nolan.

Nolan tossed the paddle to the boy and walked out of the room. This wasn't going anywhere. Those four were more likely to head the coat drive before they would get in any type of trouble.

Nolan still had his old schedule, so he looked down to see where he should head to next. At this point, he needed to meet as many people as possible, so he decided to go to class: Fitness for Life with Porter. Well at least it's a class I can keep up in.

The bell rang. He saw some boys with gym bags, so he followed them to the locker room. Nolan didn't have any clothes to change into, but he didn't care. The one thing he looked forward to, other than being undercover, was being able to participate in P.E. He was a gifted athlete in high school, and he got to relax and have fun for at least one period a day.

He left the locker room and stepped into the gym. The bleachers were folded in, but he'd never seen bleachers go so high in a high school gymnasium. There were eight basketball hoops and a separate section for the volleyball team. "Wow, nice gym," Nolan said to himself.

"Yeah, it's something else, isn't it? Lot of good memories on this court." Nolan spiraled to his left and recognized Ken the hall monitor in gym clothes.

"You monitor the gym too?"

Ken laughed, "You know it. Coach Porter told me to warm the class up and send them to the football field."

"Why are you hanging out in a high school, Ken?"

"I'm trying to get my teaching license. Until then, I've been hired to do odds and ends around the school . . . hall monitor, teacher's aide, assistant football coach. I'm the Red Rock High School renaissance man."

"Some might call you a renaissance man . . . but you seem more like the super senior to me."

"Maybe you might be on to something. I do love the potato bar here."

Nolan smiled. "I can't wait to try it."

Ken gave Nolan a thumbs-up and blew his whistle. He made the class run around the gymnasium three times, do some stretching, and sent them out to Coach Porter.

While they made their way up the reasonably steep hill to the football field, it finally dawned on him that Coach Porter was the same man who badgered Nolan in the parking lot. He arrived at the field and wandered over to Coach Porter. Nolan stuck his hand out to him and introduced himself. Coach Porter didn't take his hand but, rather, pointed to the line where the other kids were paired up throwing the football around.

"Find someone and warm up," Porter said.

Nolan eased over and watched Karen playing around with some of her friends. He tried to slink over there to grab her attention. He intercepted a pass from Karen and gave her a huge smile.

Karen gave a slight smile back. "That's not fair. I didn't know you were trying to intercept my pass."

"It wouldn't have mattered if you did."

Karen decided not to fake a smile this time. "Too bad we won't see if you could intercept me without cheating. Coach Porter is never going to let you play in jeans and a weird eagle shirt."

"I think I'll be fine. I know how to deal with loser gym teachers. Especially guys who couldn't hack it in Texas."

"How did you know he's from Texas?"

He didn't want to give too much away as to why he was there and how he'd already gotten information about one of the teachers from Principal Bitton. It might blow his cover on the first day. "Uh, that boy I played video games with. He told me."

"Why would you call him a loser?" Karen asked.

"He chewed me out for something as stupid as parking in the teachers' lot. There aren't any signs. He acted like a real ass."

"Good to know. I'll let my dad know what you think of Coach Porter."

"Why would your dad care about what I think of Coach Porter?"

"Because they're the same person."

Karen grabbed the football and ran to the others. For the rest of class, Coach Porter broke them into four teams. Nolan took a deep breath to calm down. All he had to do was play football for the next hour. Nolan noticed Karen talking to Coach Porter, and he could only assume the worst about what Karen told her father. He did his best to ignore them, but he would sneak a glimpse every now and again to see if they were still chatting. A million thoughts raced through his mind, and there wasn't anything he could do about it.

Nolan put his head down and did his best to get through the rest of the day without any more distractions, embarrassments, and stupidity. The whistle blew to end class. He started to race back to the main campus when he felt a tap on his shoulder. Like a bad dream, Ken stood there with red gym shorts and a white tank top. "Coach wants to talk to you after class."

Nolan took his time getting back to the locker room. He knew Coach Porter was waiting for him, but that didn't mean that he had to talk with him. Nolan crept into the locker room and grabbed his bag without being noticed. He tiptoed by the coach's office and blended in with some of the other students leaving. He made it out of the locker room without talking to Coach Porter. This was the first thing that went right all day.

Nolan checked his schedule. His stomach growled, and thankfully he had lunch next. He contemplated whether to go and grab something to eat from the cafeteria or go back to his grandpa's house. He took a deep breath and ducked out of the school. He wanted to grab a beer, sit back on the couch, and watch SportsCenter. He could start over fresh with his new schedule the next day. Karen came in the door Nolan was exiting. He did a one-eighty and followed her to the lunchroom. His twenty-three-year-old hormones decided it was best to grab a bite to eat before heading home for the day.

Nolan got in the line that Karen was in. With a knot in his throat and butterflies in his stomach, Nolan said, "Is the lunch here any better than dog food?"

"Oh yeah, we have Gordon Ramsey as our school chef. I think today he's serving a prime rib or lasagna; it's really a true delicacy."

"Ha," Nolan laughed nervously. "About your dad . . . well, what I meant to say is that, uh . . . I guess I didn't know he was your dad. I would've never said those things about him."

Karen's icy stare shook him to his core. "I get it. You think he's an ass, but you wouldn't have said it to me if you knew he was my dad."

Nolan paused. He didn't know what to say, but he knew he'd had enough of this bullshit of a day. "Yeah, that sounds about right. Your dad flipped out on me about a parking space. He's an ass."

30

"You think he flipped out on you?" Karen asked. "I heard exactly what he said to you. He told you it was a teachers' lot and you needed to move. You think he flipped out, and I think you're a drama queen."

Karen turned her back on Nolan. Her face burned hot, and her ears pinned back like a pit bull right before they attack. Nolan thought it would be best if he let her cool off. He backed away, but Karen wasn't finished. "Another thing . . . my Dad doesn't like being blown off. Next time he sees you, and there'll be a next time, you should go ahead and be a man and talk to him."

Nolan tucked his tail between his legs and went towards the parking lot. He'd forgotten what high school was like—the halls filled with bratty kids and the classes with over-educated snobs. Nolan realized he'd wasted his first day. The only people he had conversations with were the student body officers, a football coach, and a hall monitor slash super senior. This wasn't the way to do his job. Nolan had got caught up trying to fit in with a high school girl that he thought was hot. This wasn't who he should be forming relationships with. He needed to get close to stoners, jocks, and goths—anyone who might help him make a bust and get the hell out of Red Rock High School.

Tomorrow was going to be his first day all over again. It was time for him to do his job. He knew he was a better cop than this. How could he let a high school environment throw him off of his game so much? Nolan had been in life and death situations that he handled better than a sassy girl. He had to refocus and come up with a game plan.

# CHAPTER 5

Nolan stormed into his Grandpa's house and went to the kitchen. He snagged the loaf of wheat bread and a jar of mayonnaise. He slammed the turkey on the bread and slathered the mayo all over. By the time he finished making his sandwich, it looked like it had been run through a blender.

"What did that turkey ever do to you?" Jared laughed. "What are you doing home so early?"

"Not the best first day, but I have a plan to make tomorrow more productive."

Jared lowered his head, "You mean to tell me you didn't have a plan today? You were just winging it out there?"

"Well, sort of," Nolan said. "But that's not going to happen tomorrow. I know what needs to be done."

"Son, ever since your mother died, I've done the best I could to look out for you, and now I'm going to give you an important piece of advice. Pull your head out of your ass. You need to take the next weeks, maybe even months, to discover, execute, and finish the job you were assigned. If you go in guns ablazing, you're going to keep coming home from work at lunch."

Nolan knew that his grandpa didn't have faith in him, and it made his blood boil. He goaded his grandpa into an argument. "Things may have worked like that in the 1930s, but today kids need instant gratification. I can find a stoner behind the bleachers, offer him a better product, and bam, he introduces me to his dealer."

"Your big plan is to catch a kid smoking and have him bring you to his dealer? I don't mean to be rude, but that plan sucks. If it were that easy, they wouldn't need a cop to go spying around the school."

"What would you do then?"

"I figured I would have to repeat myself since you don't listen. Keep your big mouth shut and your oversized ears open. People like to talk about themselves, and they really like it when someone listens to them. When people like you, you make friends. When you make friends, you get invited to social gatherings, when you get invited to these gatherings, then you find the drugs."

"Grandpa, who calls parties social gatherings? I was joking about you and the 1930s, but if you keep talking like that, I'm going to have to ask you to get your zoot suits out," Nolan said.

Jared gave a loud and agonizing sigh and left the room. "Wait!" Nolan yelled, "I obviously need a new plan of attack. If you say to listen, then that's what I'll do."

The following weeks at school, Nolan was like a ghost. He showed up to class on time—with a schedule that wasn't made for Einstein—he kept his mouth shut in the lunchroom, and he even managed to stay out of Karen's way. After third period, he went to grab a slice of pizza from the à la carte when he felt two eyes piercing the back of his neck. Nolan tried to look out of the corner of his eyes to see who was there. Coach Porter stood in line behind him. This was the first time he'd seen the coach since he blew him off. Nolan slid off to the side and out of line.

"Are you always this big of a wimp?"

Anyone and everyone knew that deep, raspy Texas drawl. Nolan didn't know what he was going to say to him, but Coach Porter was right. He acted like a complete wimp. Nolan turned to him. "I don't know what you mean."

"That's your story?" Coach Porter looked at him as if to say you've got to do better than that.

"I didn't do anything wrong." Nolan was in disbelief that the coach wouldn't let it go. He wondered if Coach Porter had ever looked in a mirror. Not many people on earth would want to have a one-on-one conversation with this bear.

"I never said you did. I wanted to know if you were interested in playing football, but I don't want a candy ass on my team." Coach Porter grabbed his salad from the à la carte and strode off down to his office.

*He wanted me to play football?* He jumped up and pumped his fist in the air. Karen didn't tell her dad what Nolan had said about Coach Porter. This was the best news that Nolan received since he arrived at Red Rock High.

Nolan floated towards his locker when a group of kids in the weight room were grunting and cheering.

He poked his head inside the room. He saw needles, testosterone, and human growth hormone inside one of the open gym bags. Nolan's skin about jumped off his body. This was the exact opening he had been looking for. It wasn't cocaine, meth, or weed, but a steroid bust in a high school that would make the news. He went into the weight room, grabbed four 45-pound plates, and put two on each side of the bench press. He gripped the bar, slid the bar exactly in the middle, and lifted it off the rack. The bar dropped on him like an anchor as he struggled to get it off his chest.

With the bar firmly cemented to his chest, Nolan did the only thing he could think of. He rolled his body to the right so the weights would slide off the bar. As he rolled over and the weight slid off the right side of the bar, the left side of the bar shot up, and the momentum of the weight threw Nolan off the bench. Nolan popped up quickly and played it off cool hoping no one saw him. Everyone in the weight room had his eyes glued to Nolan. The roar of the laughing from the others in the weight room was booming. Nolan picked up the weights and made a break for the door. Suddenly someone shouted for Nolan to stop.

"There are sixteen guys in here, and you didn't ask for a spot?"

Nolan kept his back to the kid and said, "I didn't want to bother anyone's workout."

"Well, you did a hell of a job of that. Jerry over there is still on the floor busting a gut."

Nolan looked over to see a big meathead laying on his stomach pounding his hands on the ground laughing louder than any human should. Nolan faced the boy, and he took a step back at how massive this kid was. His shoulders looked like they ate his neck.

"You're a high school student?" Nolan asked. "I've seen Mr. Olympia participants with smaller muscles than you."

"That's the look I'm going for." He flexed his pecs. "Chicks did the big ones, if you know what I mean. If you want to really start working out, we're here every day. You can swing by and have a proper spotter for your lifts. I'll even teach you a thing or two."

"Sounds fun; I'm in," Nolan said. "What's your name?"

"My name's Torrey, but people call me Juice."

"Why Juice?" Nolan asked

"I'm six-foot-five, 230 pounds of beautiful, black muscle. Naturally people think I'm on steroids—otherwise known as "juice." Someone once said I have more juice in my body than Jack Lalane, and that's where the legend of Juice was born."

Nolan thanked Juice for the invite and assured him that he would be there tomorrow after school. Nolan could hardly drive home fast enough. He couldn't wait to tell Jared the good news. This was going to be his first bust into what was sure to be a long and successful life of busting scumbags undercover.

# CHAPTER 6

*T*he following day, Nolan roamed the hallways all day. He poked his head into the weight room as he walked by, making sure Juice wasn't in there already. Nolan had been smiling like a schoolgirl all day. Lifting would not only get him back in shape, but he could set his plan in motion and get the drop on these oafs before Thanksgiving. Juice claimed he wasn't on steroids, but nobody on planet earth walked around with the base of their neck bigger than their head without being artificially enhanced. If Juice couldn't come up with a better lie than that, then Nolan already had his bust in the bag.

He went into the weight room after school and, sure enough, Juice and his band of protein guzzlers stood by the squat rack. Juice was behind one of the smaller kids with his hands under his armpits. The kid started squatting, and Juice went down with him on every rep. Nolan was mesmerized as this 125-pound kid went down and up five times with 305 pounds. He had more than twice his body weight, and he threw it up like nothing was on the bar. On the sixth attempt, his knees started shaking, and the weight was too much. Juice grabbed him under his armpits and helped him finish the squat. Juice turned around, looked right at Nolan, and yelled at the top of his lungs, "That's what a spot looks like! Don't let me catch you without a spotter again, dumbass." Nolan felt like flipping him off, but he nodded his head in agreement.

"I'm new to this weightlifting game," Nolan said. "Maybe you can teach me a few things."

"Hell, son; I'll do you one better. You're going to jump in with our routine."

Nolan paused. He wasn't in the mood to try and put three hundred pounds on his shoulders and go down and up with it. "I don't want to lift that much weight. I don't think I can get that much weight off the rack."

Juice took the plates off the bar and re-racked it with 135 pounds. "Good thing the weights go on and off. Now get your skinny ass over here. You'll be working with me today."

Nolan threw his gym bag down and raced towards the rack. Juice had the kind of personality that made people gravitate towards him. Nolan knew this was the mark that had a link to illegal steroids. Even Nolan was perplexed why he was so eager to please him. Juice was a natural leader, and the way he was a mountain of a man, he obviously had a great work ethic. It takes great patience and dedication to build the kind of muscle that Juice had, even with steroids.

Juice stepped behind Nolan in the squat rack. "Alright boy, you ever squatted before?" Juice asked Nolan.

"Sure, but it's been close to five years."

"So you started lifting at twelve or something?"

*Shit*, Nolan thought. He couldn't believe he had said something so stupid. What seventeen year old hadn't squatted for five years? He was about to give away how old he really was. The next words out of Nolan's mouth had to be the best lie he'd ever come up with, or his investigation was over before it even got off the ground.

"I've never squatted in my life. I was trying to impress you."

Juice got a glow in his eye like he had accomplished a great feat. "I can respect that, Nolan. A lot of people try to impress me, but it takes more than words."

There it was. All Nolan had to do to get close to Juice was stroke his ego and tell him he was the man every once in a while. Juice may have had the upper hand when it came to brute strength, but Nolan had the upper hand in intelligence. He had figured out Juice, and now he was going to milk him.

Juice showed Nolan proper techniques so he wouldn't paralyze himself and a few tricks on how to explode from the lower position. Nolan, being a former athlete, had squatted plenty of times before, but the difficult part was pretending like he'd never squatted before. He needed to look like a novice so Juice would be none the wiser. Nolan understood that deception was part of going undercover, but he didn't realize it wasn't just words. His actions needed to be more deceiving than his words.

Nolan put his shoulders under the bar. He raised his legs and lifted it off the rack. With only 135 pounds, it was far too light for him. It was more taxing on his body to stay in character than the weight was. Nolan started to descend with the weight and put all of his pressure on the balls of his feet. He tilted forward and almost lost the weight.

"Whoa, stop right there," Juice screamed after one repetition. "First of all, you need to stay on the heels of your feet. Getting on your toes is a good way to snap your spine. Put all the pressure on your heels, stick your butt out, and keep your eyes focused on something above eye level. Then go down and up without rounding your back."

Nolan executed the lift exactly how Juice told him to. Juice kept a close eye on Nolan with a proud fatherly look on his face as if to say, "I'm a damn good teacher."

Nolan lifted for a couple of hours with the crew, and he even cracked a few jokes with the guys. He left the weight room smiling from ear to ear. Before Nolan got to his car, Juice yelled out to him, "The first rule of the weight room is there's no flip flops allowed." Nolan looked down and saw the albatross. *Flip flops . . . how could I have been so stupid?* He looked up to apologize to Juice. Juice laughed and gave him a don't worry about it look. And with that, Juice disappeared into the school.

Nolan got in his car, revved the engine, and tore out of the school parking lot. He pulled into the driveway and bolted into his house. Jared was at the kitchen table sipping a cup of coffee. Nolan sat down next to him, and before Jared could ask about his day, Nolan babbled about how Juice had taught him how to do a proper squat, how he relaxed for the first time in over a month, and his embarrassing moment with his flip flops. Jared nodded his head, but he had a glazed look in his eyes wondering why his grandson told him about the friends he made. He finally broke his silence.

"Nolan, you're acting like a fifteen-year-old girl who got asked out by the Homecoming king. I don't care about your new friends."

Nolan scrunched his eyes and tried to stare a hole in Jared, but before he could say anything, his grandpa continued on. "You're there to do your job as a police officer. Why on earth are you so anxious to get approval from these kids? You were already once popular in high school, now it's time to grow up. You can't go back to the snot-nosed punk you were in high school."

"I'm doing my job. I need to make friends to get them to sell me drugs," Nolan fired back.

"That's a load of bull and you know it. When I was the chief, my best undercover agents didn't make friends with their dealers. How many people want to hang out with their tweeker who sells them dope?"

"It's a different situation. It's not dope; I'm trying to get them to sling steroids."

"Okay, Nolan. I've spoken my piece and you know where I stand. Pretend you're their friend. Don't become friends with them. Making a bust is always better when it's not a friend. I've seen agents get too close to their marks, and it never ends the way you think it will."

# CHAPTER 7

*K*aren woke up early to be alone in the student body office before school. She needed to go over a few of the last-minute details before the Homecoming dance, and if she heard any more lame love ideas from the other officers, she was going to kick them in the face. She was organizing her list when two men's voices came booming through the walls. She peered out of the crack of the door, and Juice and Ken looked like they wanted to rip each others' heads off. Karen inched the door crack open a little more to get a better view of them.

Ken was screaming at Juice. "I don't need a soldier! I have more than enough of those. I need a general. I need someone who can take care of shit when I'm not there. Any idiot can sell. I need someone who is going to grow the company."

Juice got up into Ken's face. He towered over him and yelled back. "I don't take orders from a super senior trying to be a teacher at the school where he went to high school. You don't have enough life experience to yell at me. I know how to lead. I got half the football team to quit and follow me into weight lifting just like you asked me to."

Karen clinched her jaw tight. Her dad's job depended on winning, and her ex-boyfriend and an assistant coach got the best players to quit. Was Ken trying to become the head football coach? Was Juice doing this to get back at her for breaking up with him? She fell onto the couch and laid her head back. She grabbed her head, and everything began to get blurry. She rubbed her temples to get some relief from the pain that felt like a knife was in her head. Her eyes were starting to get heavy. She laid back and buried her face in one of the couch cushions.

Karen felt a tap on her shoulder. Looking up, Nolan hovered above her. From the first time he crashed her meeting, she couldn't stop thinking about how cute he was. Waking up with him by her side wasn't the best thing she'd ever experienced, but it wasn't too far behind.

"Don't mind me poking around, but I have to wonder what you're doing sleeping through first and second period?" Nolan said.

"Are you serious? I had no idea I fell asleep. The last thing I remember is I had a massive headache. I couldn't focus, so I plopped down on the couch."

"Must've been a nasty headache, or maybe even a migraine. I saw you sleeping before the first bell rang. I just assumed you had your alarm set. What are you doing sleeping in this room anyway?"

"I didn't plan on it. I overheard something that got me woozy, and I kind of just passed out after it."

"What could you have heard that would've made you faint?"

"I don't want to say. I need to talk to my dad first."

"Come on, Karen. If it messed you up that bad from just hearing it, you need to get it out in the open. I'm a good listener and I can keep a secret. Besides you can't tell me you have a secret so good it made you pass out and then not tell me. I'm going to be a thorn in your side until you tell me."

"Okay, I'll tell you; but if you break my trust, I'm going to have my dad break your face."

"I don't think your dad would hit a student. He'd get fired, and then what would he do?"

"I think he might risk it for you. He told me if he could go back to being seventeen for one hour, the only thing he would do is kick your ass."

Nolan gulped and stood up. He had no idea that he had gotten on Coach Porter's nerves that badly. Sure, he smart mouthed him a little bit when they first met, but it wasn't that bad. And maybe Nolan had the spine of a jellyfish when Coach Porter wanted to meet with him, but was that enough to warrant a grown man wishing he could go back in time and beat him up? Nolan shook his head and snapped out of it.

"Now, what's so juicy, Karen, that you can't think straight?"

Karen sat up on the couch. "Do you know Juice?"

"Yeah, I started to lift weights with him yesterday. Seems like a good dude."

"He's not; trust me. However, I saw him talking to Ken about some sort of business that he had going on. He was really enraged by the lack of work Juice put into his job."

"Wait, what? Juice works for Ken?"

"I don't know, that's what it sounded like to me, but that's not the important part. I heard Juice say that he got the best players on the football team to quit. I know why Juice would want to hurt the team. I dumped him, and now he's trying to make it so I'm miserable. He knows that when Daddy loses he's unbearable to be around. What I can't figure out is why Ken would go along with it? Dad takes his frustration out on Ken when they lose."

"Who cares if Juice got half the team to quit? Didn't they make it to the 3A semifinals last year?"

"You don't understand. Daddy likes it here. After what happened in Texas, I don't want him to keep fighting for shit jobs."

"For a coach's daughter, you don't have the first clue about sports. Your dad wins games. As long as he doesn't screw a student, he'll be just fine. I don't know much about high school football, but I do know that Texas and Utah are a world apart. If he could make it in Texas, than Utah shouldn't be any trouble at all."

"Thanks. You're a sweet guy."

Karen grabbed her backpack, stood up, and gave Nolan a quick peck on the lips. Before Nolan could react, she was out the door and down the halls.

Karen's smile lit up the hall as she skipped to her next class. She didn't have any idea why she was having these feelings for Nolan, but she knew that he made her smile whenever she saw him, and that was good enough for her. She didn't know if she would pursue anything with Nolan. Whenever she thought about going out with him, she could hear her Dad's gruff voice. "You like that prissy little thing? I got shoes tougher than that kid."

One thing Karen always knew growing up a coach's kid was that the clichés were going to be countless. Maybe that's exactly why Karen liked Nolan. She had had enough of the jocks and the tough guys. She needed someone who could take her out other than to a stadium on Friday nights.

A good Utah boy may be just the thing she was looking for. Heaven knows that she tired of the liars, thugs, and "bad boys" that she had made a habit of dating. The first person she met when she started classes at Red Rock High was Juice, and she dated him for six months, despite telling herself that she was going away from that jock when she left Texas.

Karen spotted her Vice President and best friend, Christy, going into the SBO room.

"Christy," Karen yelled. Christy turned around out of the room and put her finger up to her mouth.

"I'm fifteen feet away, you don't need to scream."

Karen skipped over to her. "I've figured something out about me today."

Christy stared at her, "What would that be?"

"I'm crushin' on Nolan, and I'm going to ask him to Homecoming."

Christy shook her head. "The same Nolan who was an ass to me—your best friend, mind you—and the guy who was too big of wimp to talk to your dad?"

"Yeah, that's him. Don't you think he's so cute?"

"No, I don't; I think he's a tool. Anyways I thought you were done with the troublemakers?"

"No, I'm done with the bad boys."

Christy smiled. "You're exhausting."

Karen put her arm around Christy. "You love it. Besides I want to have what you and Cory have."

"We do have it pretty good. I just need to get him to stop chilling with Juice. Now *he's* a total tool."

Karen settled her head on Christy's shoulder. "If anyone knows how big of a tool Juice is, it's me."

If Christy could get behind Karen and Nolan, anyone could. Since Karen moved to St. George, she told Christy everything. Christy was more than a best friend to Karen. Growing up in Texas, she ran into trouble with the crowd she was a part of. They would sell their souls, and bodies for that matter, just for another shot of tequila, weed, or blow. Karen headed down a dangerous road, and she was still on it when she came to Utah; but Christy changed that for her. Instead of pot, there was green Jell-O. No time for booze when she taught her how good homemade root beer was. There was no reason to find the party every weekend when she could explore Zion National Park. Everything about Christy was healthy, and Karen had never seen anyone as peaceful and joyous in her life.

Karen always loved how Christy and Cory teased, talked, kissed, and loved each other. When Karen closed her eyes at night, she dreamed about having someone to do that with. Cory and Christy had been in love since they were in elementary school when they would pass notes and hold hands. Karen just knew that Nolan would be that guy for her. She just had to convince Nolan of that.

# CHAPTER 8

*K*aren and Christy made their way to the lunchroom. They found their regular table and sat down. It was on the east end of the quad, and they had been sitting there since the previous year. It has become a pseudo-popular table. Anyone from jocks to goths, geeks to freaks, and anyone in-between was welcome to sit with Karen. Cory and Juice found their way to the table. Cory stood behind Christy and wrapped his arms around her neck.

"Hey, cutie. Long time no see."

As much as Christy and Cory were in love, Karen couldn't help but think of Beauty and the Beast when they were together. Christy had long, blonde hair, a tight, fit body from cheerleading, and deep, ocean blue eyes. Cory had long, greasy, black hair that he pulled back in a ponytail, a short squatty body that made his muscles seem out of place, and an ugly ratty beard that hadn't been shaved or groomed since the previous winter.

"You saw me last night, silly."

"Yeah, but that wasn't in the biblical sense."

Karen stuck her finger in her mouth and loudly gagged.

Cory sat down next to them. "Always lovely to see you, Karen. What does my boy Juice have to do to get a second chance with you? You're all he talks about, and it's irritating the hell out of me."

Karen shifted in her seat and looked over towards Juice. "When he loves me more than his protein shakes, maybe we can have that conversation."

Juice kissed his bicep. "Dumbbells will never leave my side; dumb hoes, on the other hand, are a dime a dozen."

Karen froze. She didn't have anything to say. Juice always had a silver tongue, and that's probably why he would end up selling used cars for a living. Christy, also known for her quick, witty comments, chimed in to defend her friend. "She's just being nice to you, Juice. She has no desire to get back together with some steroid-abusing, small-balled loser like you anyway. She has her eye on some tall drink of water."

Cory looked at Christy with a puzzled look on his face. "What or who is a tall drink of water? There's no way he could be any better than my main man, Juice."

Christy smiled and stroked his arm, "He's not as good as you my little chia pet."

"I feel bad for whoever has to follow in my steps." Juice once again flexed his bicep. "Who can live up to this?"

Karen rolled her eyes at him. "It's Nolan. He's sweet and not bad to look at."

Cory laughed loudly and embarrassingly to where other tables were staring at them. "The kid who couldn't get the bar off his chest? That guy is a featherweight, and he's going to follow the champ?"

Christy slapped Cory across his arms. "Stop."

"That's alright. I've been with the champ." Karen held her finger and her thumb about an inch apart looking right at Juice. "He's not so big."

Juice kicked the chair away from the table, grabbed his water bottle, and threw it at Karen. Karen fell to the ground and grabbed her nose as the blood started to rush from it.

Christy rushed to Karen's side and examined her. The bridge of Karen's nose was crooked, with a cut right across the middle of it. "I think her nose is broken!"

"I told her never to disrespect me. I've told her and told her. Sometimes action is needed. Bitch won't ever be disrespecting me again." Juice turned to walk his little victory strut when he spotted Nolan sprinting towards him. Juice threw his fist up and prepared for Nolan.

Nolan ran right past Juice and came to a sliding stop next to Karen. He put his arm under her body and lifted gently to stand her up. "Get up, Karen. You don't want to swallow that much blood." He put her on a chair and looked at Christy. "What the hell happened here?"

Christy mumbled something, but between how fast she talked and the sheer panic on her face, Nolan didn't understand a word she said. "Christy, you need to take a breath, and tell me what happened."

Christy tried speaking again, but inaudible words came out, so she just pointed at Juice. Nolan wanted to pull the handcuffs out of his bag and haul him off to jail right then and there for assault. But Lou wouldn't be too thrilled with simple assault as a reason to blow his cover. Nolan crouched down to Karen. "Do you want to go to the hospital?"

Karen leaned into Nolan and whispered, "Go get my Dad." Nolan rushed down to the locker room knocking kids out of the way as he maneuvered through the lockers. He burst into the coach's room. "Karen broke her nose, and maybe more. There's a lot of blood. She's in the lunchroom." He could hardly get the words out from panting so hard.

Coach Porter booked it out of his office shoving Nolan out of the entryway. Not saying a word, Nolan chased behind him, but he couldn't keep up. Coach Porter erupted through the lunchroom doors screaming, "Where is Karen?" He looked around, but he couldn't see her. He grabbed Cory by his polo shirt collar. "Where the hell's my daughter?" Cory's quivering hand pointed toward the main office.

He kicked the office door open and saw Karen sitting upright on the couch with her head in-between her legs. He sat down beside her and gently lifted her head. "Who made her put her head in-between her legs? It's not a simple nose bleed. It's a broken nose, you idiots." He scooped his daughter into his arms and carried her to his car.

# CHAPTER 9

*A*fter school in the weight room, the chatter was about Karen and Juice's fight. Nolan lifted with a few of the other beginners on bicep curls. Every so often he could feel Juice glaring at him, but he kept his head down and kept lifting. A broken nose wasn't going to affect the way Nolan did his job. He felt bad for Karen, but he couldn't get caught up in high school drama. There wasn't any sane reason for him to go toe-to-toe with a psychopath like Juice. If Juice's "roid rage" wasn't proof of him on steroids, then Nolan didn't know what was.

Nolan chatted up one of the sophomores on the weightlifting team when he heard that rough, spine-tingling voice shooting through the room. "Nolan, get your scrawny butt over here." He checked out the entrance, and, sure enough, Coach Rocco Porter was engulfing the doorframe. Juice and Coach Porter locked eyes. Juice smiled at the coach with the biggest, sleaziest serpent grin Nolan had ever witnessed. Coach Porter took a few steps inside the weight room. "How 'bout I knock that shit-eating grin right off your face?"

"Do it, tough guy. Then you will have the opportunity of getting fired in Texas and Utah. That should look good on a resume."

"I can always go back to laying sheet rock, and right now it would be more than worth it to kick your ass up and down the halls."

Nolan stepped in front of Coach Porter and blocked his view of Juice. He knew he couldn't stop these two bulls from locking horns, but maybe he could distract them long enough so they wouldn't have to. "What's going on? How is Karen?"

She fractured the bone in her nose like expected, but the good news is, she always wanted to get the bump shaved off. Now they can do it while they're fixing the other stuff."

"She needs surgery? Did she tell you what happened?"

"Yeah, she told me. I even took it to Principal Bitton, and that fat tub of goo told me that nobody saw it happen. So that arrogant jackass assaults my little girl and gets away with it. That's why I wanted to see you. You saw it didn't you?"

"No. I saw Karen grab her face and let out an ear-piercing screech. That's when I ran over to her."

Coach Porter pulled Nolan in real close to him, placed both of his hands on the top of his shoulders, and looked him dead in the eye. "You need to go do something about this, if you catch my drift."

Nolan looked back at him and replied, "No, I don't. This is a problem between you three. I need to keep my head down and work hard."

"I should've known you'd be gutless. I didn't even want to bring it up to you, but Karen said you'd defend her honor. Silly me that I thought a giant wimp like you would do anything about it. The sad thing is, you're not even a small guy. You've got to be six-foot-four-inches and over 190 pounds. You look pretty athletic, but when it comes down to it—as they say in Texas—nut-cutting time you always find a way to show your true colors."

Nolan wanted to scream at the top of his lungs. *You think I'm scared of a two-bit, roid monkey like Juice, or I'm afraid to join your football team? I've been tortured by maniacs, had a gun pointed in my temple, lost my mom, and I watched my dad split on me.* But he didn't say any of those things. Instead he calmly said, "I'm sorry; I can't get into a fight. And from the sounds of the stories I've heard, you shouldn't be offering anyone as a bounty? That's what got you in trouble at your last school."

Coach Porter rubbed his hand along his beard a couple of times. Nolan took a couple of steps backwards, and he realized he went too far. Coach Porter clinched his jaw and spoke firmly through his teeth. "If half of what you've heard about me is true, wouldn't you want to stay on my good side?"

"I can't do it. You don't understand. If there was something I could do, then I would do it. I'm not afraid of that meathead and his band of ribeyes, and I certainly would love to go toe-to-toe with him, but I can't do it. I've stood up to nasty people in the past, and Juice doesn't rank in the top ten."

Coach Porter knocked on the brick wall of the weight room and left. Nolan stood alone in the doorway. He stepped out into the hallway and watched Coach Porter leave up the stairs toward the parking lot.

Nolan went back to his workout when he overheard Cory talking to Juice. "He told Porter that he's not afraid of you. You need to show him who the biggest dog in this school is. You need to stomp him out."

Nothing good could come from Nolan if he stayed in the weight room. He snuck out back to the hallway. Juice, Cory, and the rest of his hangers-on all followed him out into the hallway. Juice and Cory both got six inches from Nolan's face. Nolan took two steps back and Cory stepped forward, not giving Nolan any room to breathe. Nolan spun around and tried to walk away, but Cory grabbed the back of his hoodie and yanked him to the ground. Nolan sprung to his feet. Cory shoved him as he got up. Nolan stumbled, but he kept his balance.

Cory went to bull rush him, but Juice grabbed him in a bear hug and whispered, "Just wait a few minutes while I scare him."

Juice turned around and put his arm around one of his crew. "I hear you're not scared of me. I can understand that. And I realize everyone has to get a beating before they can truly be scared of someone. Sure, I can intimidate a few freshmen, but after I beat someone to a bloody pulp, and they avoid the senior hall just so they don't have to see me . . . that's when they are terrified just to see me. That's the feeling that I crave. That's what lets everyone know I am the big dog around here."

Nolan burst out laughing. He laughed so hard his side started hurting. He tried to respond, but he couldn't contain his laughter. He couldn't believe that someone said that. "You're telling me . . ." Nolan spit out between laughs. "So you're telling me you have a memorized speech to intimidate me? Man, you are more pathetic than I could've ever imagined." Juice tried to jump in, but Nolan cut him off. "When was the last time you beat someone to a, as you say, bloody pulp? Your muscles, your tats, your walk, your name . . . it's all fake. Just like your beat downs."

"The last time I made someone bleed? Two hours ago in the lunchroom." Juice flexed his shoulders up into his neck, "and these are pretty damn real, if you ask me."

Nolan turned serious. "Yeah, well I'm not a hundred-ten-pound girl, and as far as those impressive traps go, it's a little easier when there are growth hormones and testosterone flowing through your blood. I guess the tradeoff for large traps is a tiny dick and zits all over."

"Your little mouth just cost you big time, boy." Juice turned to Cory and motioned with his hand towards Nolan. "Finish what you started."

Cory dashed forward, lowering his shoulder and ducking his head as he tried to tackle Nolan. Nolan side-stepped, leaving Cory grasping air. "It's a good thing you quit the football team. Coach Porter would've cut you if he saw that."

Cory dove at Nolan's legs and tried to wrap them up. Nolan sprawled out, stonewalling Cory at the point of attack. "That was decent form, but just too slow. I think you need to try out for the wrestling team. It will help you with speed." Cory stood up, walked over deliberately, and threw a punch at Nolan's temple. Nolan ducked without breaking a sweat. "You need to stop. You've tried three different attempts, and obviously you can't lay a finger on me. The last thing I need is to get into a lame schoolyard fight at the flagpole."

Cory grabbed Juice's water bottle that was sitting on the table just outside the weight room. It still had Karen's blood on the outside of it, and he rocketed the bottle at Nolan. Nolan tried to catch it, but it came too fast and hit him in the stomach. He fell to one knee and gasped for air. Cory stood over him. "I don't need to try out for the wrestling team; I'm already the pitcher for the baseball team."

Cory grabbed Nolan by the collar and pulled him up to his feet. Still gasping, Nolan, out of desperation, racked his fingers in both of Cory's eyes. Cory let go of his shirt, and Nolan went on the attack. He threw a savage punch that made a loud thud right into Cory's eye socket. Nolan could feel his face sink in, and he knew he had shattered his orbital. He grabbed Cory by back of the neck and ran him headfirst in to the lockers. Cory was limp on the floor, making groans that nobody had ever heard before.

Juice sent a couple members of his clique to scrape him off the floor. Juice and Nolan stared a hole through each other, neither one wanting to break eye contact first. Finally Juice gave him a slight nod and then pointed at something behind Nolan. Nolan turned around to see Ken standing behind him.

"You need to go to the office."

"What for?"

"You literally beat Cory down to the point where he had to be helped outside. He couldn't stand on his own two feet, and you're wondering why I'm sending you to the office? What goes on in that mind of yours?"

"He came at me. I was defending myself."

"That would be believable if you had a scratch on you."

"He threw a water bottle at me. It had to be close to eighty miles per hour. It knocked the wind out of me. I couldn't breathe."

"You know who would love to hear this story? Principal Bitton. You can go see him on your own, or you can skip out on him—the same way you did to Coach Porter—and I can tell him. If you choose to skip out on him, all roads lead to expulsion."

If Nolan got expelled, his career in undercover would be over. Lou would never trust him again, and his mother's and grandfather's reputation would be tarnished because of him. "Alright, I'll go see Bitton. But he came at me. Ask anyone here."

Ken looked around at the people who witnessed the fight and smiled. "I hate to break it to you, son, but none of these guys are going to back your story up. Juice owns all of them."

Ken was right. All of the kids who saw the fight were all on the weightlifting team. None of them were going to flip on Cory and Juice. Nolan was up Shit River, and his only lifeline was Principal Bitton.

Nolan walked slowly to the main office. Eventually he would arrive, and his fate would be determined, but it didn't have to be right that second. Ken followed behind at a short distance. He followed Nolan to the principal's office to make sure he turned himself in. Nolan knew what type of guy Ken was. Ken was the guy who loved high school a little too much. While the rest of his class went on to college, careers, or adventures, Ken is working at the school from which he graduated. He may have tried a few odd jobs, but in the end, he was always destined for P.E. teacher and all-around laughing stock.

"I'm going to the office, bro. You don't need to walk me there." Ken followed even closer. Nolan walked faster. He looked like an old man at the mall trying to get exercise. Ken kept pace. Nolan picked up the pace to a jog down the red and white hallways. Ken jogged right beside him. Nolan turned on his burners and went into an all-out sprint. Ken caught up to him without any difficulty. Nolan stopped and screamed, "What the hell is wrong with you?"

"I'm just doing my job."

"Following me around? Somehow I find it hard to believe that's in your job description."

"I have a lot of jobs—football coach, hall monitor, student, and some other things—so the fact that you're in my halls gives me the right to follow you, and that's part of my job description. Besides I wanted to see if I was faster than you. Once you started your power walk, I knew I would be in a full-blown race eventually."

Nolan shook his head, "You're a weird dude, Ken."

Ken bowed to him, confirming Nolan's evaluation. "I am who I am, but that's better than leading a double life." Ken pointed to the office. "You're here."

# CHAPTER 10

Nolan had gotten used to being in the principal's office. He knew being undercover would take him places he'd never thought he'd go, but being called to the principal's office wasn't what he had in mind. He scanned the hallway from the main office. There were a few kids with bathroom passes, but most of the kids were in class or ditching school. He sat back in a chair outside of the Principal Bitton's office and rocked back and forth. *Bitton wouldn't suspend me, would he? He was the one who called Lou and wanted to flush out the drugs at his school,* he thought. Nolan knew he had to play nice so he wouldn't be kicked out of the school or, even worse, fired.

Principal Bitton slid the door open a couple of inches. "Nolan, you can come in." Nolan walked into his office and shut the door. He sat down and listened to what Principal Bitton had to say. "You don't need to sit. This won't take long."

Nolan kicked the chair away and stood straight like a marine in front of his drill sergeant. "Go see Lou. You getting sent to my office is a dog and pony show for everybody's benefit. I don't want you in this school anymore, but I want the drugs out of it. I think you're an arrogant prick, and I've put up with it because I thought you would get the job done. So you're going to take a few days off like your suspended, go talk to your boss, and if he thinks you're making enough progress, you can come back. If you're not, then consider this our last conversation."

Bitton pointed towards the door for Nolan to get out. Nolan left slowly down the halls to the parking lot. He got into his car and sped away. While he drove down the I-15, he was taken aback by the beauty of Southern Utah. The red mountains that towered over the backdrop of St. George were breathtaking. He pulled off the next exit and sat at a local park, where he watched a young man rock climbing up a steep cliff. There was a group of college kids with their wakeboards out, ready to go riding at Lake Powell. There was a mother pushing her son on the swing set. This place was one of a kind. An hour south, and Nolan could be out on the lake all year long getting sunshine. An hour north, and he could snow ski half the year. This was his city, his life, and his career, and he had to get the drugs out of Red Rock High School before they spread to the kids of his city. If they spread too far, he wouldn't get to enjoy the greatness that was his hometown.

Nolan knew he had to face the music, so he left the park and went to his precinct. He approached Lou's office and knocked. Lou called him in, and Nolan sat down. "I know I screwed up, Lou. I know that I have to change to be a better cop. That's all I've ever wanted. I want to be known like my grandpa or my mom."

Lou took a sip of his coffee. "How's the case coming along?"

"I know Juice and his crew are the one's dealing steroids. I think he may be looking for another right-hand man since his might be out for a while."

"That's what I wanted to talk to you about, Nolan. You can't go assaulting minors. I should throw you in jail right now."

Nolan fidgeted around in his chair. "It was a classic case of self-defense. I walked away, but he pulled me back by my hoodie on my sweatshirt. I avoided him for as long as I could. If someone would have told me he had a fastball like Randy Johnson's, I wouldn't have tried to catch the bottle."

"You're lucky that weird hall monitor saw the entire fight and reported it. Where are you with Juice?"

"I know he's using steroids, we know he has to have a supplier, and we know he needs more muscle to protect him. I think that's where I can come in."

Lou scoffed at him, "You, the muscle? It's one thing beating up high school kids, it's another thing being the enforcer in a drug cartel."

Nolan felt the fire racing up his face. "He's selling to high school kids, and they all saw me take down Cory. I'm going to be the enforcer of that school."

Lou loosened his tie. "Alright, say you do become the enforcer, what makes you think steroids are worth this trouble? Some kid punches a hole in the wall, his balls shrink, or he gets a gigantic head . . . why do I care?"

Nolan picked up a chair and slammed it down. "They're linked to depression and suicide, but if you think Juice is only using steroids, then you're not half the cop my grandpa says you are. Juice runs that school. I don't even think Principal Bitton can control him."

Lou picked his chair up and put it back upright. "I see it's taken a couple of years, but you figured out how a cop should think. You found one of the users, now it's time to find out if he's a dealer. You need to set a plan in motion, execute it, and live with the results. Learn to adapt, figure out what Juice needs, have him come crawling to you. Then, and only then, will you gain his support.

Nolan left his precinct with a renewed sense of urgency to crack the case. It was time to become Juice's friend, no matter what it took. The only person living that could understand what he needed to do was his grandpa, but Nolan grew tired of his lectures. This time he had to figure out what to do on his own.

# CHAPTER 11

Nolan tore into his driveway. He had the radio blasting so loud the windows in his car vibrated. He shut the engine off and slid out the driver side window. Jared sat on the porch with the newspaper open to the business section. "You know I hate that rap music. Why do you have to blast it so loud?"

Nolan sat down next to Jared. "It's Tupac. He's one of the best musicians of all time."

Jared folded up the newspaper and tucked it under his arm. "How did your meeting with Lou go today?"

"It may have been the best thing to happen for the case."

"Yeah, Lou told me you seem to have turned a corner."

"I want to do this on my own. I need to do this on my own. I can't always come to you for help."

"Seems like a selfish thing to say."

Nolan stood up. "How is it selfish? I don't want to burden you with my caseload. You should enjoy your retirement . . . not have to babysit me."

Jared put his hand on Nolan's shoulder. "I know your desires. You want to be a better cop than me or your mother. You don't want to be compared to us. You want to be in your own stratosphere. I get it, I truly do; but what you don't understand is that I never went into a job thinking I have to be a better police officer than anyone. I put my nose to the grind, and I busted my butt. Anyone who gets into our line of work for the glory or fame is going to end up dead."

Nolan sat back down and put his head on the porch pillar. "You don't understand what it's like to be in your and Mom's shadows. I get looks from the older crew, and I know they're thinking, "This is Jared's grandson and Kerry's son?""

Jared sat beside him and wrapped him in a bear hug. "I made plenty of mistakes on the job, and to be frank, my daughter would still be alive if she didn't make a fatal mistake. I worked my entire life walking a beat so my family could be something better. I wanted you to be a lawyer. I wanted your mother to become a vet. Being a cop is hard, and you can't have anything distract you. I've seen good cops lose control trying to be the best. I love you, son, and it doesn't matter what you do out in the field. Please remember that."

Nolan patted Jared on the back and went inside. He went to his bed and collapsed in it. He opened his nightstand drawer and opened up his mom's fairytale book. His mom used to read the book to him when he was a little boy, and it was the only thing that gave him perspective. He opened the book to his favorite tale, *Hansel and Gretel*, when suddenly a plan to become

Juice's enforcer hit him like a ton of bricks. It was risky ... but if it paid off, it would be his masterpiece, and the boys at the precinct would have to give him his respect. It was too bad that he had to wait three days to get back to school.

# CHAPTER 12

*A*fter his suspension, Nolan strolled back into the
school like he ran the place. He could feel the eyes
on him, and he flourished and thrived on it. He knew
when he passed by a sophomore in the halls, they were
going to whisper about how he was the guy who beat up
Cory.

He saw Juice standing by his locker with a group
of kids. Cory was in the middle of them, and he'd seen
better days. Nolan couldn't tell all of the damage he did
to him because he had sunglasses on, but that was a
sure sign the he had two black eyes. Nolan could tell his
cheek was swollen from his first punch he landed. Nolan
brashly walked right into the middle of the group.

"Juice, what's up, brother?"

Juice eyed him up and down. "Not much, man. Are
you sure you want to be doing this on your first day back
at school?"

"I'm not doing anything. I need a minute to talk to
you."

Juice grabbed his gym bag and started walking toward the weight room. "Can you walk and talk at the same time?"

Nolan ran after him. "I want to take over Cory's role in your gang."

"We don't have a gang, Nolan. We don't meet in back alleys and wear certain colors. We're a team. We get together and lift heavy shit off the floor."

Nolan stopped in his tracks. His entire plan hinged on them being a gang. Nolan's experience with gangs and the way they worked was what he was banking on. In a gang, there's a CEO, managers, and employees. If Cory had been the muscle of the company, Nolan had a fighting chance to be promoted over him. If they were a team, then it was going to be more difficult for them to drop a teammate. Nolan knew better than most that they would rally around their fallen competitor and lift him up.

"What do I have to do to take Cory's spot on the team?"

"You shouldn't piss me off so much. You're really starting to become a giant thorn in my side. You should also squat more than 135 pounds. You'll never be able to be an important part of the team if you can't lift. Look at the way Cory's built. He's like a tank. Short arms, huge shoulders, and massive legs; he has the perfect body to put up a lot of weight. He doesn't have to move it too far to complete his rep."

Nolan found his opening and launched his Hail Mary. "I'm not talking about his spot on the weightlifting team, more of his spot as bodyguard for you and the steroids you peddle."

Juice didn't even flinch like Nolan had expected after dropping the bomb that he knew that he was dealing steroids. Juice kept moving toward the weight room. He went inside, sat down at the bench press, and pulled out a syringe and a bottle of testosterone. He stuck the needle into the top of the bottle and pulled on the syringe. He filled it up, tapped it a couple of times, pulled his pants down, and stuck it into his butt.

"It always burns a little, but my gains are incredible. So you want to protect me from the big bad wolf, is that what you're saying to me?"

"You're damn straight it is. How often do you have to collect money on a late payment, or bust someone up for shorting you? I could be that guy for you."

Juice pulled out a black bandanna out of his bag and tied it on his head. He grabbed his Converse Chuck Taylor high top shoes and put them on. Juice wore those shoes while he lifted. He claimed being closer to the ground helped his deadlift. He wouldn't wear any shoes at all if that was allowed in competitions.

"What makes you think that I need a guy? Do you think that I can't handle myself if it gets out of control?"

"No, Juice, I know you can handle yourself; but I figured the reason you and Cory hung out so much was because he was your enforcer. I mean, he looks the part. It's too bad that he actually couldn't beat himself out of a wet paper bag."

"Actually, when you beat him like he stole something, it was the first time I'd seen him lose a one-on-one fight. He usually grabs a hold of the dude he's scrapping with and throws them over his head. He gives them a few shots to the temple while they're on the ground and the fight's over in the blink of an eye. I knew when you stuffed his takedown that Cory was in for an ass whooping. You had a reach, speed, and technical advantage over him."

"When he chucked that water bottle at me, I saw double for a second. I didn't know if I was going to be able to recover from that."

"You did, and that's what makes me so intrigued by you. A lot of people would've quit and took their beating, but you found a way to overcome that. If you want to be my guard, you're going to have to earn it."

"How?" Nolan asked

"You need to fight me."

Nolan put his backpack on the floor and took his shirt off. He stood above Juice. Juice stood up and took his shirt off. Nolan saw what looked like a bullet hole in his shoulder. Juice shook his arms loose like a boxer does before a prize fight. He slid into the bench and put up 225 pounds fifteen times. He sat up from the bench. Nolan clinched his fist and put them in front of his face ready to go.

"Relax, Nolan. If you want to take care of my dirty work, I'm not going to fight you for it. I wanted to see if you would fight me, and you clearly will. I guess congratulations are in order. You're my new brawler."

Nolan picked up his bag and put his shirt back on. He went out into the hallway and collapsed by the wall. He took some deep breaths. His body was still shaking form the adrenaline flowing through his blood, but he accomplished something with the case. He was going to be the right-hand man to the dealer.

# CHAPTER 13

*K*aren loved sleeping on her side, but with an ice pack and gauze stuffed up her nose, she was forced to sleep on her back. Whenever she tossed from side to side, she couldn't breathe. The doctors did a good job of reconstructing the nose, but she hadn't been back to school since Juice had broken it. The first couple of days after the surgery, her face felt like it had been bashed in by a baseball bat. By the time the pain started to taper off and she thought she could go back to school, she realized her raccoon eyes weren't going away. Karen never thought of herself as superficial. She never wore jeans that cost more than twenty-five dollars, she never had expensive jewelry, she was most comfortable wearing her SBO sweater with a plain T-shirt and her Nike tennis shoes. But the thought of going to school and having Nolan see her like this wasn't even remotely on the table. She would've forgiven Juice for wrecking her nose before she was going to show the world her grotesque face.

She had heard about the fight between Cory and Nolan, but so many rumors were floating around she wasn't sure what was true and what wasn't. Christy had told her that Nolan sucker punched Cory from behind, but Christy and Cory had been dating for a long time, and of course she was going to take his side. Karen didn't want to probe deeper with her best friend about why her boyfriend got beat up by her crush. Her dad told her that Nolan was a "pretty good scrapper," but she didn't know exactly what that meant. Juice even sent her a text message about how tough Nolan was. Everyone seemed to have told her what happened except Nolan.

Karen sat up from her bed and yelled down to her dad, "Daddy, can you come here?"

Ever since the broken nose, her Dad spoiled her even more than he already did. He poked his head in her room, "What is it, pretty girl?"

Karen loved when he called her that. It wasn't that she wanted to hear that she was pretty but that she was still her daddy's little girl. "I was wondering if you knew how to get in touch with Nolan? I heard he got suspended, and I wanted to cheer him up."

"How many pain pills did you take? He's been back at school for a few days. And from the looks of it, he seems to be adjusting just fine from suspended life."

Karen clutched her stuffed hippo that her dad gave her as a present when she was seven. "Well, don't you have a list of students' phone numbers? I would still like to get ahold of him."

"Why would I have a list of sixteen-, seventeen-, and eighteen-year-old numbers?"

76

"Why do the teachers have faculty meetings every week? You guys talk about the same thing every meeting."

"I'm not sure what you think goes on in the faculty meetings, but I can assure you we don't get the telephone numbers of our students. If anything, you would have better resources to find his phone number than me. I'm fairly certain that the list of students, and the best way to contact them, is in your student body president planner that Principal Bitton gave you at the start of the year."

"I've already checked that. Nolan Smith isn't listed."

"I think I know a way for you to get it. I'm not so sure you're going to like it, though."

Karen threw her hippo to the side and jumped out of her bed. "What is it?"

"He's been hanging around Juice a lot ever since he got back to school. Juice probably has his number."

"He beat up Juice's best friend . . . why would they be hanging out?"

"You should know better than anyone. Juice really doesn't care about who his friends are just as long as they are useful to him. Nolan beating Cory up didn't get Juice angry, it gave him another enforcer. In Juice's twisted mind, he didn't see his best friend getting an ass whipping, he saw another chess piece to his game."

Karen picked up her phone, flipped it around a couple of times in her hand, and then placed it back on her nightstand. She paced back and forth in the hallway. She stopped in front of the hallway mirror and felt her nose. She couldn't press hard, but it was healing up nicely. She walked back into her room and texted Juice, "Do U have Nolan's phone #?" She put her phone down and waited for Juice. She turned the TV on and tried not to watch her phone. After a few minutes, she went into the kitchen to get a root beer. She left her phone on the bed. When she came back to her room, she saw there was a text message waiting for her. "435-810-1572."

It was 9:15 p.m. She dialed the first six digits of his number three times before she finally hit call. She hung up the phone really quickly and turned it off. She turned her TV on and watched Jimmy Fallon.

Her phone vibrated. She turned her lamp on to look at it. It was a message from Nolan. "Juice says you are asking for my number."

She sat up against her headboard and wanted to say something clever back, but she responded with, "That's a big ten-four, buddy." She didn't know why she sent him that, but there was something about Nolan that got her all jumbled inside.

"Bo Duke called, he wants his catchphrase back," Nolan replied.

Karen did a quick Google check on the name Bo Duke. The picture of Bo popped up and Karen burst out laughing. "That was stupid. How's school? Do you miss me?"

"I can't complain. I'm doing better now that I'm allowed back in it."

Karen walked over to the window and opened it. "I'm texting by the moonlight. No matter what you're doing, it's always sexier when the moon is involved."

"I'm looking at the moon too. That's the best part about the moon. Even if you were in Texas and I was in Utah, we'd still be looking at the same moon."

Karen's heart melted, and Nolan had her in the palm of his hand. "I didn't know you had that depth in you."

"Trust me, Karen, when I tell you there are many things that you don't know about me. I love talking to you because it pulls me away from reality for a few moments, and I can just be me."

"Like what?"

"I have to go. But I'll see you when you get back to school, or maybe I could take you to lunch or something a little sooner?"

"Well, if you insist, I would love to."

Karen hung up the phone and jumped face first into her pillows. *Ouch*, she thought as she lifted her head and touched her nose gingerly with her hand. Her mind drifted to a million different places. She hadn't had butterflies in her stomach in such a long time she almost forgot what it felt like. When she started dating Juice, she never had them. She dated him because he's who everyone thought she should date. Nolan was different. Everyone she told that she had a crush on Nolan told her it was a horrible idea to start dating him. He was the mysterious man who showed up and ruffled a few feathers. Nolan wasn't her bad boy, but he wasn't her choir boy. He beat up her best friend's boyfriend, argued with her dad, and looked like a model. This was going to be a wild ride for Karen, and she planned to enjoy every minute of it.

# CHAPTER 14

*Juice* waited on the bench for Nolan to finish his last
set of clean and presses. Nolan dropped the weight
and flexed his bicep looking in the mirror. He nodded in
satisfaction.

Juice went over to the mirror with him. "Well it's not
a noodle arm anymore, but it ain't this." Juice flexed both
of his biceps and his shoulders. His neck disappeared
between all of the muscles.

"Of course mine aren't as big as yours. I've only
been working out for a month, and your name is Juice
for a reason." Nolan hovered over the weight platform
envisioning cleaning 215 pounds. He gripped the bar
firmly, straightened his back, and pulled up. He got it to
his waist, but he wasn't able to throw his body under it
to complete the clean.

"You're never going to lift that much with the bar that
far away from your body. Keep it close and explode." With
all of the faults that Juice had, he sure was an inspiring
weightlifting coach. He knew just by watching someone

do one lift what they were doing wrong and how he could correct them. "Roll the weight close to your shins and pop it up. Shrug your shoulders, drop your ass, and squat it up." Nolan tried again, but his body wouldn't listen to his mind. The weight fell to the floor.

"You'll get there," Juice said.

"I want to get there quicker. I just wish there was an easier way. You know, like that magical elixir that everyone else is taking."

"There aren't any shortcuts to success. If that's what you're looking for, steroids isn't the answer. The only way to get stronger is to keep lifting clean or enhanced. Besides, you don't need to get that much stronger. I don't need you to be strong. I need you to be tough. Your instincts are what set you apart. The way you handled Cory was a work of art."

This was uncharted territory. Juice never mentioned the fight before. "Cory lumbered around like a big moose. He lost the fight more than I won it."

"Boy, you're not giving yourself enough glory. You put a beating on him, and it wasn't really close at any point of the fight. Cory's a tough son of a bitch. I've seen him take down some dangerous guys in my day, and you put him out."

"Dangerous? I'm not so sure that word applies to Red Rock High students." Nolan rolled his eyes at Juice.

"Ain't nobody saying nothing about these candy asses at Red Rock. I'm talking about real-life situations."

Nolan grabbed Juice by the arm. "What real-life situations has Cory come across? Somebody stare his girl down at the Burger Stop? Did he and Ken, the super senior hall monitor, get into a shoving match? Maybe he went down to Vegas and tried to get into a casino." Nolan let go of Juice's arm. "I've known this community my entire life, and Cory doesn't come from the school of hard knocks."

Nolan went outside into the hall. "Wait," he heard Juice scream. He turned and looked over his shoulder. Juice caught up to him. "So what if Cory isn't from the hard life? He still had my back time and time again, and I didn't even ask for it. And for your information, getting in a shoving match with Ken is a big deal. You may not know it, but that has some serious consequences. You should open your eyes as to what's going on around you, boy."

"Why don't you open them for me?"

"Come by my mom's place about eleven."

Juice turned the corner and went outside. Nolan continued down the hall. He walked by Karen's locker and stalled. He paced back and forth between halls waiting to run into her. His phone buzzed. It was a text message. "Where are you with the Juice case?" Nolan double-checked to see it was, in fact, Lou. Nolan didn't realize Lou knew how to send a text message. He hadn't heard or thought about Lou since the fight.

"I'm his new muscle. I'm going to his house tonight. I think I'll find out about the drugs tonight."

"Good. Keep me posted. Stay away from the coach's daughter. You have a job to do."

"I'm not messing around with her."

"Bullshit. Just do your job. I have eyes and ears everywhere."

Nolan turned off his phone and waited next to Karen's locker. The drugs were going to have to wait until tonight anyway. He could always do prep work, but striking up a conversation with Karen was priority number one right now. He heard a shrill, high-pitched voice that could break the trophy case. "Can I get in my locker?"

Sure enough, there she was. The one bad thing about Karen is that she came with Christy. "Has anyone told you that you have the voice of a meadowlark singing in the morning, Christy?"

"You're blocking my locker, so, like, move."

"That time of the month?"

"Get the hell out of here, you ass. I have no idea what Karen sees in you?"

"How does it feel to not be dating the big man on campus anymore, Christy? Ever since I took your boyfriend's manhood, you seem to be a little bitchy."

"First of all, you didn't take anybody's manhood, and secondly, he's not my man anymore."

"You dumped him because he got beat up? That's cold, even for you."

"No, I ended it with him because he stood by and watched Juice break my best friend's nose."

"Spin it anyway you want, but the facts remain. You and Cory dated for years. I beat him up, and you ended it," Nolan said.

Christy nudged Nolan out of the way and put her books into her locker. Nolan gave her a smirk and raised his eyebrows. He waited by Karen's locker until he realized she wasn't coming anytime soon. He grabbed a sticky note out of his pocket and wrote her a note. "Karen, sorry I missed you. Call me when you get this."

Nolan overheard Karen in the lunchroom say that she thought handwritten notes were the sweetest thing a guy could do. Nolan could score some brownie points with her. He still didn't know how Juice felt about the two of them hanging out so much. His goal was to stop the drugs pedaling through Red Rock High, not to get a girlfriend. Tonight he was going to tell Juice that he started dating Karen and hope for the best. Juice was his whale he needed to get, but if he could have a fling with Karen while fishing for his whale, that would be even better.

Nolan took his time standing in front of Juice's front door before knocking. Juice's front yard wasn't anything like Nolan pictured. There was a small pink bike with training wheels lying flat on the very green grass. With the drought in Southern Utah, nobody had green grass; lawns weren't something that a lot of people in St. George took pride in. Watering your lawn in a drought was very expensive. Nolan loved a green yard and yard work. Both of the garage doors were open. It was a little messy, but there was a new, yellow Ford F-250 truck in the right side, and a maroon Lexus SUV in the other.

Nolan tapped on the door lightly. It was late, and he didn't know who was awake. He waited for a few minutes, and no one came to the door. He pounded with the side of his fist on the door loud. The porch light turned on, and Juice answered the door. "Come in, you're a little early."

Nolan entered the house. The wood floors had a new layer of polish on them. Nolan took his shoes off at the entrance and slipped on the floors. Juice laughed and reached his hand out to help Nolan up. They turned the corner into the living room area where Juice's parents were watching a basketball game on a sixty-five-inch flat screen HD television. Nolan immediately recognized the man on the couch. That was Judge Ed Jordan. Ed was known around the precinct as an easy lay off criminals, give them a second chance type of guy. Nolan pulled his beanie as low as it could go on his head, and looked down at the floor. He'd met Ed before, but only briefly. His heart racing, sweat pouring down his face, Nolan blurted out, "How are the Jazz doing?"

Juice's mom smiled a sweet, loving smile at him. "Not good. Portland has way too much speed for our boys to keep up with."

Juice slapped the back of Nolan's head. "You don't interrupt during the game. That's why they have time outs. My mom and Ed take this serious."

Nolan didn't know if he should apologize for interrupting the game or keep his mouth shut because it wasn't at a timeout yet. He didn't move a muscle and started to rub the back of his head. Juice hit harder with an open hand than most people do with a closed fist. The judge stood up and slapped the back of Juice's head.

"You don't treat a guest in my house like that."

Juice laughed. "Where do you think I learned it from?"

All three of them began to laugh. The man stuck his hand out to Nolan, "I'm Juice's stepfather, Ed."

Nolan shook his hand, "Nice to meet you, sir."

"Who are you calling, sir? I'll slap the back of your head if you call me that again. Your honor or king will be just fine."

Juice's mom threw a pillow at Ed. "Just because you're a judge doesn't mean everyone has to address you as one." She turned and spoke to Nolan. "Don't deem a word either of those two says to you as true. I'm the only sane one in this household. You can call me Kelley—not mam; don't ever call me mam."

Nolan waved at her. "I'm Nolan, Juice's friend."

Ed yanked the beanie off of Nolan's head. "How do I know you Nolan?" He was sure that Ed recognized him from the time they had met at the precinct. If that happened, the case was dead. Nolan held his breath for Ed's next words. "Are you the one who beat the shit out of Cory? Pardon my French."

Nolan exhaled. "Uh, yeah, that was me."

"Good. That kid has needed a beating for a long time."

"Ed, you can't say things like that about high school kids," Kelley said.

Ed turned toward his wife. "I'm not on the bench. I can say whatever I want in my house. That kid's a jerk, and if I was twenty-seven years younger, I would've crippled him."

Nolan quickly changed the subject. "You're a judge, Ed? That's pretty awesome."

Ed's smile stretched across his entire face. "Oh yeah, it is cool. Some of the stuff I get to hear on a daily basis is more entertaining than any comedy club."

"Don't nobody want to hear your judge stories, Eddie," Juice said.

"That double negative tells me you do want to hear my stories. There are plenty of my stories that have plenty of good grammar in them." Ed winked at Juice.

"Ah, get out of here, you two. The game's about to start up. Nice meeting you, Nolan."

Juice went to the door that led to the basement and went down to his room. Nolan followed him. Juice opened the door to his room and jumped on his beanbag chair. "Go over to the closet and pull out my baseball bat. Nolan grabbed the bat and handed it to Juice. He pulled out a cork on the top of the bat and dumped a little bag of pot on the floor.

"Sweet, I have some left." He grabbed a homemade bong out of his backpack and loaded it up. He lit his lighter and took a hit.

"You want some?"

"No, you jackass. Your parents are upstairs, and Ed is a judge. What goes through your head? I don't think you're playing with a full deck."

"Please, you met Judge Ed. That dude is the happiest-go-lucky bro that has ever walked God's green earth. Plus, my mom is a lawyer, so I'm untouchable."

"Your mom's a lawyer, your stepfather's a judge, and you're a doper? Makes sense to me."

"Yeah, I guess you could say that. I have to give my man Eddie credit, though. That guy has some serious game. He met my mom in court. Hit on her and everything during a trial. That's an old-school player. Someone that smooth has dipped into the sticky-icky a time or two."

Nolan shook his head and sat down on the desk chair. Juice's phone rang, and he stepped out into the hallway. Nolan grabbed the hollowed out bat and peeked in. It smelled pungent for sure, but the only pot in the bedroom was in Juice's bong. He put the bat down and spotted protein powder on the desk. He opened the lid and examined it. Only protein was in it. Someone who lifted as much as Juice wasn't going to store anything in his powder; bodybuilders' powder is sacred to them. Nolan located Juice's gym bag in the back of his closet. He opened it and, sure enough, testosterone and growth hormones were tucked away in the front pocket.

There wasn't enough to make any money selling them, so they had to be his personal stash. Nolan heard the door open but didn't put the steroids away. He laid them on the desk. Juice came back in putting his phone in his pocket.

"Who was that?" Nolan asked.

"You'll see soon enough. This is the guy who is going to make you a rich man. He's on his way over. Are you ready to do business?"

"It's not Cory, is it? I don't feel like fighting tonight."

"That's funny. You think Cory wants to fight you again? That punk is scared of you. I tried to tell him everyone gets their ass beat, but he's being a baby about it. Dude told me he didn't want to roll how we rolled anymore. That's why you are my new enforcer. This dude is going to explain the business end of our friendship."

"I'm honored," Nolan said.

Juice got a text. He read it and put his phone back in his pocket.

"Alright, let's go out front." Juice said.

This must be the mystery guest that Juice alluded to. Juice and Nolan went outside and waited on the steps for him to get out. The man stepped out of his truck, but it was too dark to tell who it was. He approached

Nolan and Juice and gave Juice a hug. Nolan's jaw hit the ground.

"This is the guy who you're in bed with? I'm out if I have to work with this idiot! I can't comprehend how he could be the guy," Nolan said.

Juice put his arm around Nolan's shoulders and gave a slight squeeze. "We've been rocking together for years, and we have a smooth operation. It's perfect."

"Look how nice my truck is. Three-inch lift kit, twenty-six-inch rims perfectly blacked out to match the color of my truck, and tinted windows all over. You think I could make that much money if my only job was a hall monitor?" Ken said.

# CHAPTER 15

Nolan gazed with a blank look at Ken. The guy who had to relive his high school glory days every day of his life was Juice's supplier. Ken slipped a few dollars into Juice's hand. There was something different about Ken. He didn't have his "aw, shucks" attitude. Was he acting at school, or right here? Either way, Nolan was making progress on this case. He just witnessed an exchange of money. Nolan felt like he needed a shower. He had to stay and watch this transaction, and he couldn't even make a move on them. On one hand, he wanted to make the bust right then and there, but there weren't any drugs being exchanged. On the other hand, he knew he was on to bigger and better things. Juice and Ken both trusted him, at least enough to do business in front of him.

Nolan crept closer to the two of them. He wanted to inform them that he was ready to sell, but he couldn't come out and say it. He had to let them approach them on their terms or he was never going to get in.

Ken broke the silence. "How are you two friends? I mean you're basically trying to sleep with Juice's ex. If I was in Juice's position, I would have to plant you in the ground at least once before I could ride with you. And Juice . . . my goodness, man. He destroyed your best friend. How can you two even stand to be around each other?"

Nolan wanted to say something, but he had no idea why Juice would want to be his friend when you look at it like that. Juice spoke up, "Let bygones be bygones; and we recognized that we could do more damage rolling together than we could do apart."

Ken had a puzzled look on his face. "Is that true, Nolan?"

"I'm not looking to ride with anyone," Nolan said with air quotes. He continued, "I know your type, Ken. I've been dealing with nickel and dimers my entire life. You come here slinging passive-aggressive comments, hoping Juice and I are going to start brawling right here. Let me lay something heavy on you. Juice and I know a good thing when we see it. No matter how many comments you make, no matter how tough you act, no matter how nice your truck is, all we care about is getting paid."

"Slow down there, youngster." Ken puffed out his chest. "We're not peacocks, and I don't care how big your tail feathers are. You want to get paid? I get that we all do, but there something about you that I don't trust. I should like you. You stick it to Coach Porter by not playing football for him, not to mention you're trying to nail his daughter; you shut Christy "Loudmouth"

Perkins up; and you beat up the biggest son-of-a-bitch in the school. On the surface, you and I should get along great; but I don't like you."

Nolan stepped up to Ken, puffed his chest out, and walked around mocking Ken. "It may have a something to do with me making fun of you at every opportunity I get?"

"That's not it. I can see why you would think that, but I'm trying to give out the super senior vibe. I expect the ridicule that comes with being an assistant football coach and hall monitor at a high school."

Juice stepped in between them. "Kenny boy, I know what it is about him that you don't like."

"You do? Please share."

"You don't like Noles over here because of the goofy-ass old man shirts he's always sporting."

Nolan looked down at his shirt, and sure enough he was wearing one of his grandpa's shirts. And apparently he had been wearing them quite often for Juice to take notice of it.

Ken eyed him up and down a few times and said, "I think that is it. Why are you wearing a lumberjack flannel? It's like eighty degrees out here."

"It's my Grandpa's shirt. We're the same size, and I usually grab the first clean shirt that fits me," Nolan said

Nolan unbuttoned the flannel to his undershirt so he would look less goofy. This was the first time that he let someone, while he was undercover, get under his skin about his appearance. He wasn't sure what that meant, but he knew he couldn't get sucked up into the high school drama that seemed to follow Juice's way.

"Do I look better with my shirt unbuttoned?" Nolan asked Juice.

"Actually, yeah man. You don't look like you should be on the cover of paper towels now."

Nolan turned to Ken. "This is ridiculous. Can we get on with the business at hand? In case you forgot, we're standing in front of a judge's house. I don't feel like drawing too much attention to him."

Ken handed Nolan the keys to his truck. "Go to the back driver side door and lift the seat up. Bring me the bag of footballs."

Nolan opened the back door and fumbled around a little bit trying to get the seat to pop up. He found the right lever and pulled up on it. The seat flew up almost hitting him in the face. There was a big duffle bag full of footballs. Nolan grabbed them and handed the keys and bag back to Ken. Ken began tossing footballs out of the bag onto the driveway. After the bag was emptied, he picked up one of the footballs, yanked on it with two hands by the laces, and pulled them in the opposite direction. Nolan heard the rip of the Velcro and the football open up. Ken dumped out needles filled with steroids.

"There's thirty syringes filled with the exact amount needed to gain major muscle mass in just one cycle. You need to find at least three people to buy ten apiece. I don't care if you go to your local gym and find the smallest dork there. You have a week to sell them. There's only one small catch. You have to make the exchanges at the football games on Friday night."

"Why at the games?"

"Because someone with footballs at a football game isn't going to attract any unwanted attention; and if you get caught, it isn't going to get linked back to me. I'll be coaching."

Nolan snatched footballs and put them in his car. He started his car up and looked out the window. Ken raised both of his eyebrows two times quickly. Nolan pushed the clutch down, put it in gear, and raced away.

Juice sat on the hood of Ken's truck. "What's your read on him?"

Ken pulled Juice off of his truck. "Don't sit on my truck. He has a swagger that I like. I don't know how he'll be as a soldier. It takes someone who's willing to go to the ends of the earth and find junkies at their lowest point. We'll see how he does with the Vitamin S and go from there."

Juice scratched his face. It was a nervous tick that he'd had since he started using. "I think this is the wrong play. The only weightlifters he knows are in the high school gym with me, and I got them on lock."

"It's the right move. If he can find a couple of meatheads without any leads, then he'll be able to deal the other stuff. Like you said, the only people he knows already have steroids. He's going to have to think outside the box to sell it."

"We'll see," Juice said.

# CHAPTER 16

$K$aren stormed down the halls of Red Rock High. She shoulder-bumped and shoved anyone and everyone, including teachers, along the way. She burst through the door of the SBO room and flung her book bag at the couch. It narrowly missed Christy, who was relaxing on the couch. Christy picked up the bag and threw it back at Karen.

"What's going on, Karen, besides almost knocking me with your school books?"

Karen flopped down and laid her head on Christy's lap. "I'm sorry, sweetie. Why hasn't Nolan asked me to Homecoming yet? I've thrown out so many hints, and he doesn't seem to grasp them."

Christy put her hand on Karen's back and started to massage it. "You know I love you, right?"

"Of course I do," Karen said

"Then I say this out of love. Your hints are stupid. What have you done that lets him know that you really want him to ask you to the dance? I've heard you talk about how much fun you had last year in Texas at your Homecoming. I've heard you give your fake complaints about how swamped you were from planning the Homecoming dance, but I've never heard you say, 'Hey, I want to go with you.'"

Karen looked up. "I can't say that to him. It's the guys who ask the girls. I don't want to come off as liking him."

Christy laughed. "I don't know a lot about Nolan, but what I do know is that he won't be playing any games with you. If you want to go with him, you'll have to nail a note on his forehead that says, 'I want to go to the dance with you.' Otherwise he'll continue to miss your signals. I've got to get to class. We'll talk at lunch."

Christy exited the SBO room leaving Karen alone with her thoughts. *I can't be any clearer. I've talked to him about Homecoming. I've mentioned I don't have a date. I told him I want to go. What else do I have to do? Should I take Christy's advice and just tell him I want to go with him? Why am I crushin' on an idiot?*

Karen sprung off the couch and stormed through the door. She marched into her dad's office and exclaimed, "Dad, I need to use your computer. I need to find out what class Nolan has."

Her dad looked at her with his icy stare. "You think my computer has the list of every student's class schedule on it? You're going to have to ask a counselor what class he's in. And you better have a damn good reason why you need to see him."

"Of course, I have a superb reason to see him. Some might say it's the most important reason in the world. I'm asking him out."

Coach Porter ignored her, and he continued working on his computer. He heard Karen say his name, but he didn't look up from the computer. Finally he heard, "If you're not going to help me, then you can make your own dinner tonight."

"Oh that's alright. I haven't had Chinese takeout in a while. That sounds pretty good tonight."

Karen's voice went from confident and stern to pouty in an instant. "Please, Daddy. You wouldn't want me to miss my Homecoming dance that I've worked so hard on, would you? If I missed the dance, everyone would point at me and say, 'There's the girl who put the dance together but couldn't even get a date.' Then I would have to move to a new school or die of embarrassment."

"Stop talking, sweetheart. I love you, but you're giving me a headache with all your blubbering. He's the lunch aide right now; I'm sure you'll be able to find him in the lunchroom."

Karen smiled at her dad. "Thank you, Daddy. So you *do* have everyone's schedule on your computer? Good to know."

Coach Porter closed his eyes and rubbed the bridge of his nose. Karen bubbly-bounced out of her father's office. She heard the door locking behind her as she left. She skipped all the way to the lunchroom. Nolan ate his lunch by himself in the corner of the lunchroom waiting for second lunch to start. She snuck up behind him and sat next to him.

"You know what I hate about October in St. George?"

Nolan flinched. "Whoa, when did you get here?"

"It doesn't matter. Do you know what I hate about October?"

"No, I have no clue. Tell me what's to hate about October in St. George . . . the awesome view of the unique red mountains, the palm trees, or the great Mexican restaurants?"

"There's no fall crisp in the air. It's always so hot. It's October second. The dance is almost here, and it's still ninety-five degrees outside. And there's no air conditioning in this corner of hell."

"They really should invest in some type of air conditioning. Didn't you grow up in Texas? That has to be the hottest place in the United States."

"I grew up in Panhandles. It had nice, cool days there. This place is way worse for heat. It's that dry heat. But my tan comes in a lot nicer here."

Nolan checked her skin out, among other things. "Yeah, there's no doubt about that. You have some fantastic skin."

"Obviously you dig me, so here's what's going to happen. You're going to go buy a nice, new shirt and tie. I like a black and purple combo. I'm going to wear my pretty, new, tight black dress, and you're going to take me to Homecoming this Saturday. We're going to ride in Christy's and her date's limo."

Nolan's head spun. She was so perfect: aggressive, gorgeous, smart, and determined. He didn't want to compromise his investigation, but he couldn't resist her. "I think I would look good in purple."

"Good. Pick me up at five o'clock on Saturday night. I'll take it from there."

She stood up and gave Nolan a kiss on the cheek. Nolan couldn't take his eyes off of her. He didn't have to start serving second lunch for another fifteen minutes. He had a million thoughts racing through his mind, but the only one that mattered was, *How am I going to explain to Lou that I have a date with a high school girl?*

# CHAPTER 17

Nolan crept into the station. When he walked in, the whispers stopped, and all eyes were on him. He made his way through the office and sat down on a chair outside of Lou's office. He rubbed his hands up and down his pants and waited to be called in. He watched his coworkers do paperwork and make jokes with each other. He did miss going into the office and interacting with adults. Every once in a while someone would look over and give him a half-smile, but more often than not, they passed by without making eye contact. He hadn't been undercover that long, but not coming in every day made him the invisible man. The door to Lou's office swung open.

"Come on in, Nolan."

Nolan walked in and shut the door. He took a seat and waited for Lou to say something. The office was different than what he remembered. The paint on the walls was a darker shade of blue. Lou's desk was positioned against the back of the wall as opposed to in the middle of the room. Lou always liked to have a lot of wiggle room if he had to be stuck in an office, but now he had none with that desk positioning. He only had one picture of his daughter up. Pictures of his wife and daughter usually covered his wall. His office now had a business feeling. Not the "come on in and take your shoes off" feeling it had once portrayed.

"Nolan, you've been undercover for two months, and not much to show for it. The Homecoming dance is where a lot of deals go down, Principal Bitton relayed to me. What's going on with your investigation?"

Nolan clenched the arms of the chairs and hoped he had enough new information for Lou. "I have Juice's trust. I'm his new go-to guy ever since the fight. He introduced me to Ken, his supplier. Ken wants me to get three new people interested in buying steroids before the Homecoming game. "

"That shouldn't be hard. I'll send some of the other officers as your buyers. We have a few guys who like to hit the gym around here. They'll be perfect."

"I don't think Ken cares about meeting them. All he wants is the money."

"That's even better. Tell him you found three buyers and you need the product as soon as he can get it. We'll get him some money, stroke his ego, and then boom, bust his sorry ass," Lou said.

Nolan knew a small steroid arrest wasn't going to get his name in the papers, so he wanted more time to work. "Are Ken and Juice the guys you really want to go after? These guys seem like soldiers. Don't we want to track it back to the real dealers and see if they have real drugs? Not a smalltime steroid bust that won't do a bit a difference?

"An apprehension of two low-level degenerates isn't anything to write home about. However, making Red Rock High a safer school is something to get excited about. Get these two out of the system, and make our schools a source of community pride."

Nolan nodded his head in agreement. He stood up to leave when he heard. "One more thing, kid. I heard about your Homecoming date. I know Coach Porter's daughter is one of the hottest pieces of tail that I've ever seen, but you need to be extremely cautious. Not only are you disobeying a direct order from me, but you're dating your main mark's ex."

Nolan slid back into the chair. His stomach churned from hearing a sixty-two-year-old man call an eighteen-year-old attractive. "We haven't gone out yet. I can call the entire thing off."

Lou leaned back in his seat and put his feet up on his desk. "I want you to listen to me real close right now. Do you think I've let you roam the halls without eyes and ears on you? I've seen the way you look at Karen. You only get a chance at something special one, maybe two times in your life. If she's that, then I want you to reach for it. That's not to say if it interferes in your police work I won't pull you off, because I will. But I know what it's like to lose the love of your life, and I don't want anyone to go through that hell."

It dawned on Nolan why Lou's office only had the one picture of his daughter. He stood up and shook Lou's hand. He went out into the precinct and asked one of the uniform officers, "How long have Lou and his wife been separated?"

"About two weeks. He went home one day, and she was all moved out. Lou's been unbearable since then."

Nolan left the office and sat and stared off into the sun. Lou and his wife had been married forever. What could've happened in the past month that could make his wife leave him that hadn't happened in the previous forty years? Right then and there, Nolan decided that whether it interfered with his investigation or not, he was going to make his play for Karen.

# CHAPTER 18

Nolan parked in the back row at Budge Field. Memories of Friday nights flooded his memory. He had played once on Budge Field when he was in high school. The grass was perfectly measured and cut. Football was meant to be played on grass, and no school took better care of its stadium than Red Rock High. Tailgaters grilling up hot dogs and burgers made Nolan's mouth water. The way the freshly cut grass smelled, the butterflies in the locker room, and the coach's rallying cry before the game were the only reasons Nolan ever went to school.

Nolan showed his school ID to the ticket booth, and he entered the stadium. He made his way to the student section in the bleachers. He scanned the stadium to see if Juice was anywhere in sight, but no such luck. He maneuvered his way to the top of the bleachers. He turned to sit down, but he got shoved from behind. He tripped over the bleachers and ended up face-first in a sophomore's nachos. He sat up and used the top of his shirt to wipe the cheese off his face. For once in his life, he was thankful that the concession stand didn't heat up the pre-packaged imitation cheese. Karen put her hands over her mouth so she wouldn't laugh.

"I'm so sorry, Nolan. I didn't mean to push you that hard!"

She helped Nolan up and burst out laughing. Nolan wanted to be mad, but she was too pretty to get mad at. They didn't need the stadium lights; her smile could light it by itself. She had her hair in a ponytail, wore a white tank top and cutoff jeans, and her face had the numbers of a few of the players painted on her cheeks. She gave him a hug.

"I didn't expect to see you here."

"Why would you say something like that? I love football."

It took everything in Nolan's power not to brag about the time he scored two touchdowns in a span of forty-four seconds when he played for UNLV. He told this story to every girl he ever wanted to impress. It was his go-to move, and he couldn't even use it at a football game.

"Well, this is our fifth game, and you haven't been to any of the others," Karen said.

Nolan put his arm around Karen. "You think I would miss the Homecoming game with the hottest girl in the state as my date?"

"You're such a cornball. Those cheesy lines don't work on me."

"I would tend to agree with you if you weren't blushing."

Karen's face turned even more red, and she buried her face in Nolan's chest. He pulled the rest of her close to him and gave her a hug. The two of them watched the game together, as well as the other five hundred students at the game. It was getting close to halftime when Nolan's stomach began to grumble.

"I'm going to get something to eat from the snack shack. Do you want anything?"

"Yeah, I'm starving. Get me a hot dog and Sprite. Mustard and pickles on my hotdog."

"No ketchup? That's the best condiment for a hot dog."

Karen shook her fist at Nolan. "You Utah people like to ruin something great like a hot dog and put ketchup on it. You guys do the same thing with your fry sauce. It's known as Thousand Island to the rest of the world. And don't get me started on the barbeque scene here. I haven't had any good pulled pork since I left Texas."

Nolan shook his fist right back at Karen. "Fine, I'll bring you a dog with fry sauce if that's what you really want."

Karen turned and winked at him. Nolan was floating on cloud nine. This was more than a little crush he had on her. She had him flirting. He hated to flirt, but with her it came naturally. Nothing could bring him down.

He stood in line for their hot dogs when he heard a soft, strong voice behind him. "You seem to be getting cozy with Karen. It's all good. I kicked that hoe to the curb. You can have my sloppy seconds."

Nolan knew Juice was baiting him, and he also knew he couldn't take the bait. "If I'm going to take sloppy seconds off of anyone, I can't think of anyone better than you."

Juice pulled him to the side of the shack. "You got some cheddar for me?"

"Cheddar. That's clever since I'm covered in it," Nolan said.

Nolan reached into his pocket and slipped him the money for the steroids in the palm of Juice's hand.

Juice took his hat off, and put the money in it. "Where did you find the buyers at?"

"The police station. I know a guy," Nolan said.

Juice laughed. "You're a weird dude, Nolan, but I like your style. Not too many people have the stones on them like you do. That's why we get along. We handle what needs to be handled, and we don't apologize for it."

"I appreciate that. When do I get my cut? I'm not out here risking my neck selling drugs for free."

"Slow your roll. I don't have any say in who gets what. I'll give this to our man on the sidelines over there, then he'll give it to his guy, then we'll get paid. I have to warn you; you're not going to make the fortune you're hoping for slinging testosterone. You need to take a bigger risk to get the bigger piece of pie."

"Fine. Let's do that. I'll do what needs to be done."

Juice turned away and walked slowly toward the exit. "I can't do that, Nolan. Coach Ken doesn't trust you yet. Prove to him that you can sell the lower-end product, and then you'll get your chance."

Nolan got back in line and grabbed his and Karen's hot dogs and went back to his seat. Karen had tears in her eyes. Nolan put his arm back around her. "What's the matter?"

"Why are you giving money to Juice? Why are you even hanging out with him? He's nothing but a thug."

"I can handle Juice. He's just another pretend tough guy in a long line at Red Rock High School."

"Don't underestimate him, Nolan. I've seen with my own two eyes how violent Juice can be. It's like there's a switch in him. He pins his ears back and looks like a pit bull. When that happens, he is a very dangerous person."

"You're going to have to believe me when I tell you I'm not afraid of Juice. In fact, it's him who should be afraid of me. Why are we even talking about Juice? We should be talking about how good of a job your dad is doing tonight or the dance tomorrow. Juice should be the last thing on our minds."

Karen took out a tissue from her purse and wiped the tears away from her eyes. "It is going to be pretty epic tomorrow, isn't it?"

"You know it. Do you have anything planned?"

Karen's mouth dropped. "You're the guy. You're supposed to have all of the details ironed out."

Nolan quickly began shaking his head. "No way. *You* asked me out. The only friend I have in this school is Juice. I'm pretty sure you don't want to spend the night with your ex-boyfriend and his date."

Karen turned to her best friend Christy who sat in the row in front of them. She had been eavesdropping on their conversation and mercifully jumped into it. "I'll tell you what. We're already riding in the limo together, why don't we just cook for our dates, and then we can find a post-Homecoming party."

Karen jumped up and down. "Yeah, let's do that. I love to cook, and we won't have to deal with an entire group. Just the four of us will be so much fun."

Nolan didn't have any other option, so he nodded in agreement. *I don't like Christy, and I've never met her date. This ought to be a wonderful night,* he thought. None of that mattered to him in the end. He was going out with his dream girl, and if putting up with Christy for a night was the price he had to pay, then he would gladly pay it.

# CHAPTER 19

Nolan circled the block a couple of times before he pulled into the Porters' driveway. He had on a classic black button-up shirt, white slacks, a white tie, and white suspenders. All he was missing was a pork pie hat to complete his 1950s look. He pulled into the driveway and drifted to the door. Before he rang the doorbell, he wiped his palms down the legs of his pants.

He rang the bell and waited. He swayed back and forth, shifting weight from one leg to the other. The door opened and his worst fear became a reality. Coach Porter stood in the frame. His shoulders could hardly fit through it. Maybe it was because he was taking out his daughter, but Coach Porter's grimace seemed even more intimidating. Coach Porter stepped sideways and motioned for Nolan to come in. "She's upstairs putting the finishing touches on her makeup."

Nolan stepped inside the house. Beautiful, cherry wood floors were freshly polished. There were elk, deer, and moose mountings all over the walls, and the living room had leather couches and an old oak table with four chairs fit for kings. There wasn't a single football or sign of any sports-related memorabilia.

"I thought you would have some trophies or records somewhere," Nolan said.

"Yeah, I got those, but I just put them in the basement. That deer head that hangs on my wall is my trophy."

"Do you mind if I ask why?"

"Well, you just did. It comes down to what's the most important to me. I don't coach because I want to hold records or display trophies. I coach because I can teach life lessons, make lifelong friends, and help influence a child's life. I recently read a study that said ninety percent of CEOs in Fortune 500 companies participated in high school athletics. I don't know if that's true or not, but it's not difficult for me to believe."

Nolan sat on the couch. "Me either. I loved playing football and baseball when I was younger."

"You did? Why aren't you playing now?"

"It's just not in the cards right now," Nolan said.

Coach Porter sat in a recliner chair facing Nolan. "It doesn't matter anyways. My boys are starting to hit their stride."

"Yeah, I was at the game last night. Your boys had a great game. That zero coverage on the final play of the game was a gutsy call. I would've thought a cover two or four would've been the safer call."

Coach Porter started to rock in his chair. "That would've been a safer call, you're right. But when in doubt, send the dogs. We had a better chance of getting to their quarterback because of their depleted line. I wanted to have the ball out of his hands as quickly as possible and not give their receivers a chance to get open."

Nolan nodded his head in agreement. "As Michael Jordan said, you miss one hundred percent of the shots you don't take."

"That's the least dumb thing that's ever come out of your pretty-boy mouth since I've met you."

There it was, the comment that fired Nolan up so much he wanted to take a baseball bat to Coach Porter's kneecap. That's just the type of guy Coach Porter was. If Nolan was going to have any type of relationship with Karen, he needed to let snarky comments roll off his back.

"You think I'm pretty?" Nolan said.

Coach Porter's face looked like a volcano ready to erupt. "I didn't say that. I would never say that. If you weren't about to take pictures with my little girl, I would rearrange that face of yours."

"Oh Dad, stop the grizzly bear routine."

They both looked up to see Karen walking down the stairs. Nolan was amazed how she could walk in what looked to be five-inch heels. Her black dress fit her like a glove, and the slit up the side of the leg showed just the right amount. She had on a gold necklace that enhanced her beauty. It was the first time Nolan had seen her hair curled. He liked it, but she looked the prettiest with it pulled back in a ponytail.

Nolan stood up from the chair. "I'm not sure how to describe how stunning you look right now."

"Hey flyboy, don't get any cute ideas. She may be eighteen, but that doesn't mean she's not my baby," Coach Porter said.

Karen laughed. "Thank you, Nolan, that's very sweet of you to say. Daddy, I'm not a baby, and I can take care of pretty flyboys on my own. Besides, I'm almost nineteen. That should mean something." She winked at her dad. Coach Porter blew his daughter a kiss, gave Nolan a death stare with his bloodshot eyes, and left the room.

Karen gave Nolan a hug. "We're waiting on Christy and her date to get here. Then we'll get started."

"Who got saddled going with Christy?"

"You better be careful. She's my best friend. And if you don't want my dad to rearrange your face, you'll be nice to her."

"Noted," Nolan said. "But seriously, who is she going with now that she and Cory have split?"

"Rex Hall."

"The fullback on your dad's team?"

"Yeah, that's him. Christy wanted to go the dance with someone who could hold his own if Cory decided to cause a scene."

"Isn't he a junior? Christy likes 'em young."

Karen shook her head. "She just wants someone the exact opposite of Cory. She wants someone who isn't going to break her best friend's nose, someone who is more interested in her rather than their steroid buddy, someone who won't throw away their life for a stupid feud with a coach.

Nolan scratched his chin with a puzzled look on his face. "How'd Cory throw his life away? He's only a senior in high school."

"You felt how fast he can throw. That kid had all sorts of college scouts looking at him to play baseball, but he up and quit the team because the coach asked him not to hang out with Juice."

You could see the wheels spinning in Nolan's brain. "What does hanging out with Juice have to do with Cory and baseball?"

Karen sat down on the sofa and put her feet on the coffee table. This was particularly impressive in her Homecoming gown. "Cory would follow Juice to the depths of hell. Juice has that effect on people. Just look at you. He gives you a little attention, and now you're his new 'muscle.'" Karen raised her fingers with air quotes.

Nolan slouched back down in the recliner. He put his head in his hands, took a few deep breaths, and then looked up at Karen. "Juice is a means to an end. Kids at Red Rock are afraid of him because he's a bully, but he's just another wannabe. His stepfather is a damn judge. They live on the top of the hill. Nobody gravitates to him like you're suggesting. Believe it or not, he's smarter than everyone else in that school. He manipulates every circumstance to get what he wants."

"Is that why you hang around him? He manipulated you into being his friend?" Karen asked.

"I hang out with him for the same reason you dated him. There's nothing else to do."

Nolan and Karen retrieved to their corners much like a prize fight when the doorbell rang. Karen raced to the door and opened it. Christy and her date, Rex, were in the doorway. Nolan got up and gave Rex an awkward bro shake. If Juice was the Hercules of the school, then Rex had to be the Sampson. He was well over six feet tall. He looked like he could move his pectoral muscles on demand like Mr. Universe. Nolan liked what he knew of Rex but couldn't figure out how he got a date with Christy. Something about the kid's face didn't seem right. It might be the bug eyes or the small ears, but he wasn't someone the girls were beating the door down to date.

Karen hugged Christy. "You look so cute. I love your hair."

Christy cackled back in her high-pitched high school cheerleader voice. "You look so amazing. OMG, look at you and your necklace."

The two of them continued to compliment one another for the next ten minutes. Rex took a seat on the sofa. Nolan hated silence. He couldn't sit in peace ever since he was captured and water boarded.

"So Rex, that was a good win you boys got last night." For the first time since going back to school, Nolan felt old sitting across from a sixteen-year-old and his zits.

"Yeah, we beat them like a drum, if ya know what I mean."

Nolan scrunched his eyebrows. "I'm pretty sure anyone could've understood what you said, Rexxy. Not really hard to decipher what you were going for."

Rex sat up. "Rexxy . . . I kind of like it."

Nolan grabbed a pillow, put it behind his head, and sank lower into the recliner. It was going to be a long night if the two of them were going to be isolated for more than five minutes.

Christy came and jumped onto her date's lap. Rex wrapped his arms around her waist. He had a schoolboy smile. "What are you boys talking about?"

Nolan threw his hands in the air. "I don't know. I'm not sure of anything that comes out of Rex's mouth."

Rex leaned in closer to Nolan. "I think you need to pay closer attention."

Nolan ignored Rex and looked at Christy. "Where are we going to dinner?"

"Right here." Christy pointed towards the kitchen. "Karen's dad prepared us some of his world famous pulled elk sandwiches with potato salad and rolls. It's literally the best thing I've eaten."

*Great. I'm sure he put a little d-CON into my sandwich,* Nolan thought. With the way the night had started, Nolan was going to roll with anything. He was out with the most beautiful girl, he didn't have to think about the case for one night, and he got to tease Christy about her date.

They sat at the table, and Nolan took a bite out of his elk. It didn't taste gamey at all. It was savory, tender, and delicious. He devoured his sandwich in a few more bites. The salad had fresh potatoes in it and tasted remarkable. Nolan scarfed that down and looked at Karen. "Your dad is the best chef who has ever lived." Karen gave him a wink, as she wasn't anywhere near finished with her food.

Nolan pulled his phone out and killed a few minutes waiting for everyone else to finish their food. Rex devoured his food just as quickly as Nolan did, but there wasn't any way in hell that Nolan was going to strike up that conversation again. The limo arrived and honked the horn. Nolan went over and put his hand down for Karen. She grabbed it, and off they went.

# CHAPTER 20

Nolan took Karen by the hand, and they pulled open the basketball gymnasium double doors together. It was high school hell as far as Nolan could tell. Red and white streamers across the ceiling, awful handmade banners with the Homecoming theme "Life's the Ocean; Go for a Sail," and the football players reliving their Homecoming win from the previous night. Fortunately for Nolan, Rex made a beeline for some of the football players, so he didn't have to talk to him.

Karen and Nolan joined some friends to take their dance pictures and make plans for the after-party. Juice and his date were part of the group. Nolan wanted to have one night where he wasn't working. He wanted to be with Karen and not feel like an undercover. Crashing Juice's group put a damper on those plans. If there was one thing about Juice, it was business all the time. Nolan was sure Juice was in the process of cooking up a plan to get more of these high school kids on his steroids during the dance.

Christy pried Rex away from his friends long enough to join them for the pictures. Rex rolled his eyes at her when she told him she wanted to dance and hang with her date. After a few dances between the two of them, Rex slipped out the back. Nolan scratched his head. Either Rex was extremely shy around girls, or he liked the fellas. Either way, Christy had been leaning against the wall the majority of the night. When the DJ played an uptempo song, Karen would drag Christy in the middle of the giant group, and she would dance. However, when the slow songs began, it was her and the wall again.

Nolan and Karen had a good rhythm going on between them when Christy tapped Karen on the shoulder. "Rex has been gone for a long time. Can Nolan go look for him?"

Karen looked over at Nolan. "What do you say?"

"I'm not sure I want to find out where he is. He's like talking to a box of rocks, he won't dance with someone as pretty as Christy, and he snuck out the back."

Christy smiled and sarcastically said, "Ahh, you think I'm pretty."

Karen laughed uncontrollably for a few seconds. Nolan turned around really fast. "Fine, I'll go find him; but this doesn't mean were friends, Christy."

Nolan burst through the gym doors to the hallway. He looked around for any sign of Rex. He went to the main entrance to see if he went for some fresh air. Nolan walked out of the school and saw Cory, Juice, and Rex standing by Cory's car. They were talking intensely about something Nolan couldn't make out. Nolan clenched his fist and gritted his teeth every time he saw Cory . How he could break Karen's nose and only get suspended for three days was a mystery in itself.

Nolan casually went over to them and spun Rex around. "I figured you'd rather be playing grab-ass with the bodybuilders than dancing with a hot dime like Christy."

Rex stepped up to Nolan, towering over him. Rex stared and slapped himself in the face a couple of times. "I'll beat your ass right here and now."

Juice grabbed Rex and pulled him to the side and said, "Unless you have a death wish, Rex, you need to calm down." Juice turned to Nolan. "What are you doing out here? Shouldn't you be inside giving my ex a wonderful evening?"

Nolan loosened his tie. "You ever get the feeling you and I are going to have one hell of a brawl one of these days, Juice. I know you're using me to protect you from the small-time nickel and dimers who want to kick your ass every day, and you know I'm using you to make some quick cash. But there's so much tension between us. I don't know if it's taking your girlfriend out or beating up your other girlfriend, but something's up."

Juice grinned at him. "Nolan, I like you bro; and you might be right, there might be some un-squashed beef between us. If that's how you feel, then let's squash it right here and now. I may be mad at you for all the stuff you said, but you know me. I'm all about that cheddar. If you can bring me money, then we won't have no problems."

Nolan turned away from Juice and looked around. "Where'd Cory go?"

"Ah, you know that dude. He comes and goes as he pleases. The truth is, Rex here only asked Christy to the dance so she would have a horrible time. He and Cory set the whole thing up. Kind of a d-bag thing to do, but that hoe shouldn't have dropped him after one fight."

Nolan pushed Rex to the ground. "You're a real piece of work. The only reason Christy went out with you is because you told her you could handle Cory if he started any bullshit. Now I find out it was Cory who wanted you to mess with Christy. I should beat you so bad that your mom wouldn't recognize you."

"You don't know me." Rex reached his hand out for Juice to help him up.

Nolan gave Rex a bewildered look and threw his hands up in the air.

Juice shook his head at Rex. "Most of the time, I don't know what you're talking about, Rex, but I put up with you because Cory likes you. However, you make my dog look smart, and I've seen him eat his own crap."

Rex kicked over a garbage can and punched a window out of a blue Toyota pickup truck. Before Rex could hurt someone, Nolan asked him, "What was Cory's end game here? Was it to make Christy's night miserable?"

Rex turned to Nolan still huffing and puffing. "No, he wanted me to get her all riled up and ticked off at me. Then he said he would take care of the rest. He also wanted me to make sure I left her alone. But I didn't know how with so many people at the dance."

Juice unbuttoned the top button of his shirt. Irritated, he asked, "Why didn't you ask her if she wanted to talk in a quieter place?"

"I guess I could've. But why would I need to talk to her?"

Nolan screamed at the two of them. "Focus, Rex. Why on earth would Cory want to get Christy alone?"

Rex put his hand on his chin. Nolan could see the gears turning, but he knew they weren't going to leave first gear. "I'm not sure. He said something about a lesson plan."

Nolan's face contorted as his eye began twitching. "A lesson plan? What the hell are you talking about, Rex?"

"Cory said last night he had a lesson for her or something like that."

Juice put his hand on Rex's shoulder and, in a soft voice, said, "Did he say he was going to teach her a lesson?"

Nolan could almost see an actual light bulb turn on above Rex's head. "Yeah, that's what he said."

Juice laughed, "I'm not sure how Coach Porter gets you to remember the plays or why he hasn't kicked you square in the ass."

Rex turned to Juice. "That's easy. Danny has pictures on his wrist of where I need to go and what hole I need to hit."

Juice put both of his hands on his head and looked to the sky. "The quarterback has to show you where to go before every play?"

Rex nodded his head with a goofy smile. By this time, Nolan had burst back into the school and was screaming down the hallway. He saw Karen dancing with a group of her friends. "Karen, where is Christy?"

Karen took a big drink of water. "She went with Cory. He said he wanted to make up with her. I think she may do it, too. The way Rex treated her, Cory seems like Prince Charming now."

Nolan went back out into the hallway and scanned to see if he could find any clue as to where they went. He burst through every classroom door searching for them. He was shocked to find out how many kids left the dance to go make out in classrooms. To each couple hooking up, Nolan yelled at them, "Cory and Christy, have you seen them?"

Nobody had a clue as to where they were. It dawned on Nolan. *The SBO room has a couch on it.* He sprinted to the west side of the school and flung the door open. He saw Christy lying down on the couch. He turned the lights on and gasped. Christy was in the fetal position sobbing. Nolan crept closer to her, and blood gushed out of her nose. She had a cut above her right eye. Nolan took his shirt off and put pressure on the cut. The cut was too deep for him to stop the bleeding. Her arms had hand prints and bruises up and down them.

Nolan hugged her loosely, not wanting to hurt her even more. "Did Cory do this?"

Christy sniffled and mumbled, "He said it would be worse if I told anyone."

"You don't need to worry about that coward. His punk ass isn't coming back."

Christy put her head on Nolan's lap. "I don't know . . . I don't know what to do. Can we go home?"

"Sure. I'll have Karen get the driver to take you both back to Karen's house. I'm going to find Cory."

"No, you can't. It will make it worse if you do."

Nolan pulled his shirt off her eye and showed her how blood-soaked it already was. "No it won't, Christy; trust me. All these woman-beaters say that, but all of them need to get their asses kicked. Once they find out there's someone bigger and tougher than they are, they find a new prey."

"What if he finds me before you find him?"

"Then it will be the biggest mistake of his life. You're going over to Karen's house, and anyone who would step into Rocco Porter's house looking for a fight is leaving in an ambulance. I'm going to go get Karen now."

Nolan found Karen and took her back to the SBO room. When he opened the door, Karen screamed and burst into tears. She rushed over to her friend and wrapped her in her arms.

"Who did this, my angel?"

Nolan grabbed Christy around the waist and put her arm around his neck. He led her and Karen back to their limo. He told the driver not to stop for anything or anyone until they got back to Karen's house. He tried to give the driver a twenty-dollar bill, but he refused. Nolan patted him on the back, and the limo pulled away. Nolan stormed back inside the gym. By now the word had spread that Christy was brutally attacked. There were a lot of rumors already flying around. One of the cheerleaders asked Nolan if it was true that Karen and Christy were fighting over him. Leave it to high school to not let facts get in the way of a good story.

Nolan ran down to Principal Bitton's office and pounded on the locked door. "Lawrence, I know you're in there. Let me in; its urgent."

He heard some rustling and fumbling, then the door swung open. Bitton had a coffee mug filled to the brim. Nolan could smell the whiskey from where he stood. "What's going on?" Bitton slurred.

"Your school's drug ring has evolved into brutal beatings. It's time I take these lowlife pond scums out."

Bitton wiped the sweat off of his forehead with the back of his hand, then he wiped his hand on his shirt. "I don't care what you do as long as you clear it with Lou."

Nolan went back into the gymnasium and started eyeing who he knew that would give him a lift. He recognized a couple of the kids from some of his classes, but he never made too nice with anyone that wasn't going to help his case. He spotted Juice in the corner talking to one of the football players. Nolan assumed he was making a drug deal with the kid. He stormed over and snatched Juice's car keys out of his pocket.

"I'm taking your car to my house. I need to pick my car up. You can come with me or pick up your car later. I don't care."

Juice grabbed the keys back out of Nolan's hand. "I'm tired of you thinking you can lay your filthy little hands on me. Next time you grab me, we're going to throw down like you talked about earlier tonight." Juice looked at Nolan and shook his head. "Where is your damn shirt, Nolan? You look like a stripper."

"Funny story about my shirt. I had to use it to stop the bleeding from above Christy's eye because Cory beat her until she could only whimper."

Juice froze. All of the blood left his face, and he looked like a ghost in a snowstorm. It took him a few minutes to gather his thoughts. "Are you sure it was him?"

"Christy told me. Do you want me to get her on the phone so you can confirm my story? Or are you going to give me a ride home?"

Juice snagged his coat jacket and tossed his keys to Nolan.

"I'm a little drunk. You better drive."

# CHAPTER 21

*J*uice kept shaking his head and mumbling, "I can't believe he actually did it."

After the third or fourth time of saying that, Nolan finally blurted out, "Was this premeditated or not? It's one thing to get caught up in the heat of the moment and do something as horrible as this. If he was planning it, though, that takes this to another level."

The color had returned to Juice's face, and he spoke with a little more clarity. "Nolan, you got to believe me, bro. Cory would joke around about beating her ass, but that was all just macho talk with the boys. He and Rex were secretive about the dance, so I had a gut feeling that something was going down. I found out about the setup for a bad date five minutes before you did. Ever since you and I have been rolling together, Cory has been doing his own thing."

Nolan saw Juice's eyes. He rubbed them and lowered his head. Nolan concentrated on the highway. He didn't want to see if Juice was crying or not. "I believe what you're telling me, Juice. The only problem I have with you is that you created this punk. I don't know if 'roid rage' is a real thing. If it is, Cory has it."

"What do you mean I created it? I would never bang on a girl. My mom would have my nuts in a vice if I ever did that," Juice said.

"You mean besides breaking your ex-girlfriends nose? I guess that doesn't count."

"It's like you said earlier, Nolan. It's one thing to lose your temper and throw a water bottle. It's another thing to put your fist on them."

Nolan raised his eyebrows and stared a hole through Juice. "Whatever helps you sleep at night, Juice. I'm not saying that you told him to go and beat up women. However, the lifestyle you live led him to thinking he's a hard gangster when in reality he's just another wannabe. Sure, you guys might sling some dope and maybe a little coke, but you, Ken, and Cory are small time."

Juice grabbed the wheel, and they swerved off to the side of the road. "How do you know we've been dealing coke and pot?"

Nolan laughed as if Juice were insulting his intelligence. "I see a lot of your shady dealings every day that you don't have any clue I notice. Like tonight, I know you were dealing to that football player right in front of everyone. You think you're clever hiding in plain sight, but I see it. And Ken driving a brand new Ford F-150 on a hall monitor's/coach's salary? You have to be more clever than that if you want to be successful with deception. I once busted a dealer who had me chasing him up, down, and around. That was a clever man right there. You guys are nowhere near his level."

"WHAT DO YOU MEAN BY BUSTED?" Juice asked.

Nolan pulled his gun out of his ankle holster and badge out of his pocket. "I'm a cop, Juice, and you're officially my informant."

"Screw that. I'm no snitch. I would rather rot in the pen than rat out my boys."

"Alright, if that's how you want it. But why don't we go ask the judge, a.k.a. your stepdad, how much time he would give to an eighteen-year-old who gave illegal steroids to a cop for him to sell would get in the penitentiary, not to mention all the dope you have in your room that I witnessed you separating into dime pieces for distribution. You're facing big boy time, Juice. You're a supplier, not a dealer, in the eyes of the law. I'm offering you no time in prison. Hell, you'll still be able to walk at graduation if you help me out."

Juice scratched his head. It was a nervous tick that Nolan spotted the first time they met. He only scratched his head when he felt jammed up, and Nolan definitely had him in a bind. Juice turned with bloodshot eyes and softly whispered, "My mom's always wanted to see me walk at graduation. Alright Nolan, what do I gotta do?"

Nolan clapped his hands together. "Very good decision, Juice. We'll get squared away in the morning; but tonight we're going to find Cory."

"Are you gonna arrest him?"

"No, not tonight. Nobody saw what happened tonight, so I don't think any charges are going to stick. Tonight I'm going to kick his ass just like last time."

Juice and Nolan cruised down St. George Boulevard with the top down on Juice's car. "The Vard," as the locals called it, wasn't a dangerous place by any means, so Cory felt a lot meaner and tougher than he really was there. Nolan's favorite Mexican restaurant was there. Most nights it was dead, but Saturday nights on the Vard consisted of drunk high school jocks looking for a fight or strung out hippies looking for some pot.

There was a dingy, little bar on the south end. Nolan and Juiced pulled into its parking lot. It was a little log cabin joint with decrepit wood and missing shingles. Juice pushed open the doors and a bell rang. Nolan scanned the room for Cory. *This really is a dump,* Nolan thought. It had fake wood wallpaper; the billiards tables' felt was torn and tattered, not to mention that some of the tables were missing some of their balls, and Nolan's foot stuck to the floor from all the beer that hadn't been cleaned up. Nolan approached the bartender. He wore a leather vest and a black baseball hat pulled down low, and he was cleaning a few beer mugs. He wasn't a big guy, but he had his intimidating qualities. The knife scars on his face and arms were enough to make Nolan walk a little softer toward him. "Have you seen a muscular kid who's as wide as he is tall in here tonight? Walks like a 'tough guy'?"

The bartender spit a string of chew into a cup. "Look around, son. That's all that ever comes in."

Nolan cleared his throat. "I'm sorry, maybe I wasn't specific enough for you. I'm looking for the high school kid—who you probably serve alcohol to knowing he's a minor—because I'm going to crush him like a can. Can you help me with that?"

The bartender shook his head. "Nah, still doesn't ring a bell. I can't help you, sonny boy."

Juice stepped up to the bar. "Gerry, have you seen Cory?"

The bartender spit a string of chew at Nolan's shoes and then turned to Juice. "Cory said that this twig would be looking for him," as he pointed to Nolan, "but he didn't say anything about you, Juice."

Juice sat down at on a stool. "That's because he thinks I got his back. After what he did tonight, I don't."

The bartender poured a shot of whiskey and slid it to Juice. "You want a drink?"

Juice picked it up. "Don't mind if I do."

Nolan stood over Juice. "Uh, I mind. I need to find Cory, and that's not going to happen with you sitting here getting drunk."

The bartender opened a bottle of beer and gave it to Nolan. "You need to relax. Here, this one's on me."

Nolan slid it back to him aggressively. "Apparently you don't listen. I need to find Cory. He beat up a defenseless girl tonight, and I'm going to return the favor to him."

The bartender looked over at Juice. Juice gave him a nod as if to tell him that it was true. The bartender pointed toward a backroom. "He's back there. He said he was going to crash here tonight. So why don't you sit back, enjoy your beer, and then when the place dies down a little bit, you can go in there."

Nolan took a couple of steps toward the backroom when Juice grabbed the back of Nolan's shirt. It stopped him dead in his tracks. Juice didn't even stand up from his stool. Nolan never felt power and strength like that before.

"Listen to what Gerry told you to do. You don't want this situation to get even stickier by having a crowd," Juice said.

Nolan backed up from Juice's grip. Then he pulled up a chair and sipped on a beer. He didn't want to test Juice tonight. He didn't know if it was the alcohol or the steroids that gave Juice super strength tonight, but there was a little extra something there.

The three of them sat and made small talk until last call. A few of the locals had one last drink and stumbled out the door. Gerry threw his keys to Juice. "Lock the place up when you leave, and drop the keys off at my house before the morning." With that he walked out the door.

Juice and Nolan snuck up to the backroom and peeked inside. Cory was lying on the couch watching a movie. They kicked the door in, and Cory jumped up. "Juice, you scared the hell out of me." He looked over at Nolan. "What the hell is this faggot doing here?"

"Man, I had to roll with Nolan tonight after what you did to Christy."

Cory laughed hysterically. "That slut had it coming. She dumps me because this lucky punch legend over there connected with a few shots."

Nolan got into Cory's face. "You want to find out how lucky those punches were?"

Cory sat back on the couch. "I don't think you're going to do anything tonight. In fact, I think you're going to walk back out that door and forget that tonight happened. If you don't, you'll regret stepping through that door."

Nolan's eyes turned to stone, and his ears pinned back like a pit bull. He rushed Cory, who immediately pulled out a nine-millimeter glock and pointed it right in Nolan's face. "I told you that you're going to turn around and leave. If you don't, I'm going to add an extra hole in your face tonight."

Nolan clenched his teeth and fists. Cory stood up off the couch never taking the gun off of Nolan's forehead. Juice dashed over and threw Nolan to the ground. Cory pointed the gun at Nolan, but Juiced stepped in between them. "Cory, put that shit away. You really want to throw your life away over this punk?"

"Throw my life away? Who's going to know it was me? Anyways, it's self-defense. You saw how he attacked me, didn't you, Juice?"

"Nobody's going to believe that stupid story, man. Gerry's dumb-ass gave me the keys. You think that cops aren't going to figure out what happened if you pull the trigger?"

Cory took the gun off Nolan and waved it around. "Why are you acting like a coward, Juice? The Juice I know would have my back through thick or thin. Well, bro, it's about as thick as it can get, and I need my partner in crime back."

Juice shook his head. "You're barking up the wrong tree, brother, if you think I'm going to watch you kill someone tonight. Slinging and dealing is one thing, murdering a classmate is something I don't want any part of."

While Juice and Cory were arguing, Nolan snuck up behind Cory and sucker punched him right in the temple.

Cory dropped like a bag of bricks. He tried to stand back up, but his knees wobbled like jelly, and he face-planted on the floor. He grabbed his gun, but everything was blurry. All he could make out were shapes. He fired at anything and everything that moved. Nolan and Juice dove out of the backroom back into the bar. They bolted through the door and out to the parking lot. They were both drunk, but Nolan started the car up and squealed the tires out of there.

"We need to go see Lou," Nolan said.

"Who the hell is Lou?"

Nolan nodded his head. "He's my boss over at the precinct. This is a lot bigger than busting a couple of kids for selling dope."

Juice turned and looked at Nolan. "You better figure this out. I'd rather be in prison than be a dead snitch for you."

"Don't worry. Cory still thinks you're the king. He didn't once point that gun at you. He begged for your help to execute me."

"It's not Cory I'm worried about. Where would a kid like Cory—whose parents kicked him out a long time ago—get a gun?"

Nolan squinted his eyes on the road trying to stay in his lane. "It has to be Ken, right?"

"I don't know. As far as the drug world goes, Cory and Ken are pretty much the same person. They both talk to the kingpin directly, and they both give me supplies to sell."

Nolan gripped the steering wheel tight and put the pedal to the floor. "I thought you were the kingpin of Red Rock High? Now you're telling me Cory is?"

Juice rolled his eyes at Nolan. "I am the man at Red Rock High School, but tell me how many times you have seen Cory in a class? The only times Cory comes to school is when he missed Christy or he wanted to get a lift in. I may be the king of the school, but that kid runs the streets."

Nolan clapped his hands together and the car swerved into the other lane of traffic. "Now we're getting somewhere. I should've made you a snitch a long time ago. It would've saved me the six weeks of hell that I went through.

Juice grabbed the wheel. "You better pull over. We need to sleep this shit off."

Nolan pulled off to the side of the road and shut the car off. He and Juice leaned their seats back and closed their eyes. Juice began snoring immediately, but Nolan couldn't sleep. He wondered how he was going to explain to Lou that he blew his cover and, instead of arresting Juice, he made him an informant.

# CHAPTER 22

*Sunday* morning rolled around, and Nolan set up a meeting with Juice, Lou, and himself. He wanted to clear the air on what's going on with his investigation and also introduce them to Juice. Nolan wasn't sure how Lou would react to Juice being on the inside, but at this point, Nolan had been backed into a corner and had no other option. After the night he had at Homecoming, he didn't want to find out how Prom would end. He needed to end this quickly.

He waited outside Lou's front door for Juice to arrive. Juice arrived in an old, beat-up Toyota pickup truck. He got out of the truck with a hoodie pulled up over his head and sunglasses covering his eyes.

"Where's your car?" Nolan casually asked.

"You think I want anyone to know that I'm at a cop's pad? They already saw me and you leave together last night. In fact, if you don't want anyone to know your Benedict Arnold ass is a cop, you should be a little more incognito."

Nolan rubbed the bridge of his nose with his thumb and index finger. "You need to crack a history book. I'm not sure you know who Benedict Arnold really was. As far as me being seen at a cop's house, who knows he's a cop? If I wouldn't have told you who lived here, would you have suspected anything if you'd have seen me here? You need to relax, do this good deed, and make the world a better place. But most importantly, you need to act normal, and driving around an old beater truck isn't something you would normally do."

Nolan pounded on the door. He heard Lou trampling down the stairs. He opened the door in his white tank top and blue boxer shorts.

"What is wrong with you? Do you want everyone's attention? I thought we were meeting this early on my God-given day of rest because you wanted it to be a secret? But here you are pounding away at my door like a Mormon missionary."

"Grab your cup of coffee, Lou. You're always more pleasant when you have your liquid crack in you."

Lou waved the two of them in and invited them to sit at the kitchen table. It was an odd shaped table. It almost had the shape of a stop sign. There were six chairs spread around it, and they all looked like they were made of different wood.

"Lou, did you make the table and chairs yourself?" Nolan asked.

Lou smiled, "Oh, I'm glad you noticed. Nobody ever notices it, but woodwork is a bit of a passion of mine. I'm not terrific at it, but I love to create something from an old tree. The entire process gets my blood pumping.

Chopping it down, stripping the branches, cutting it into the two-by-six planks, and then I get to create something out of it. My favorite part is making hidden compartments, though."

Lou tapped on the post of one of his chair legs and then opened up a hollow leg containing his hidden bourbon. Lou poured some into his mug. "And you wonder why I'm always in a better mood after I get my coffee."

Nolan tilted his chair onto the back two legs. "I have to admit, Lou, that's fairly fantastic."

"I'm glad you approve."

Nolan pointed at Juice. "Lou, this is our new informant. There isn't anyone with his finger on the pulse of what's going on at Red Rock High more than Juice. He's already helped me track down Cory at one of his hideouts, and I feel he's going to be a valuable part of the investigation. I also feel like he'll be able to speed it along."

Lou sat down in the chair across from Nolan and Juice. First he looked at Nolan and spoke sternly to him. "An investigation doesn't need to be sped along. It needs time to work itself out and be done with precision. You've only been under six weeks, the middle of August to the beginning of October . . . that's it. I know you've felt like it's been an eternity, but it hasn't. I fully anticipate you being there until March or April."

Lou turned his attention to Juice. "What's in this for you? I always thought you were the prick that Nolan was after? Every update he gave me consisted of what you were doing and how you were connected to the steroids.

Even my good buddy from college, Larry, told me you were the guy that needed to get busted. And now you think I'm going to trust you to be an informant? Am I taking crazy pills?"

Juice rubbed the back of his head. "Larry? Who's Larry?"

Nolan butted in. "Are you talking about Principal Bitton, sir? Because if you are, I don't think he's the best character witness. The guy was drunk at the Homecoming dance. What kind of principal tips a few back at a school-sanctioned event? If that were one of the students, he would've been expelled and no questions would've been asked."

Lou rested the back of his head into his hands, and his mind drifted off. "Ah, the stories I have of Larry at the old frat house. When he told us he wanted to be a teacher, we were all sure he'd be one of those guys who we'd see on the news because of inappropriate behavior toward a female student. That guy loved to drink and flirt."

Nolan snapped his fingers to get Lou out of his trance. "We have more pressing matters to deal with than your trip down memory lane. One night with Juice and I found out more about the drug scene at in St. George, Utah, than I did in six weeks. I ran the idea by my grandpa, and he thinks it's a good route to go."

Lou stroked his midlife crisis goatee in his fingers. "I don't think so. I don't know anything about this kid except what you told me. I'm not going to put this case in some low-level drug dealer's hands." Lou looked over at Juice. "No offense, kid."

Juice stood up and struck his fist on the table. "You may be right about the type of kid I am. I do sell a little weed and steroids to make some extra dough. I may like to raise a little hell on the weekends just to feel more alive. I break the law. There's no ifs, ands, or buts about it. I'll tell you one thing though. I'm your only chance to clean up that school. I know Nolan's dirty little secret. One phone call and your investigation will go in the crapper. What you going to do then? Send another undercover into the school? That would be obvious."

Lou took a slow sip of his bourbon coffee. "I don't need this bust, kid. I'm helping out an old friend who said the drug problem at his school was getting out of hand."

Juice went around the table and sat next to him. "That's just it, bro. It's not just a school problem. We have an assistant football coach who provides enough steroids for the team that professional bodybuilders would be jealous. We have a kid who runs the streets selling crack to young mothers, strung-out tweekers, and students, and he beats women. You think you're only helping a friend out? You're dead wrong. Not only do you need me. I need you. I created the monster Cory's become, and now I want to help take his ass down."

Lou nodded his head. "Alright, son. I didn't think there was any way you could convince me of letting you help out. But I'll tell you something, Juice. Not only can you help out, but you need to turn your life around and help this department out full time."

Lou patted Nolan on the back. "Your mom would've been proud of you today. It would've been easy to take

Juice down for a few petty crimes, but you dug deeper and made the right call as a police officer. That's growth."

Lou went through the procedures with Juice of when and where to meet Nolan with information. They needed to appear as if nothing had changed between the two of them. Nolan was still Juice's new muscle, and Juice still ran the school. When they were finished going over a few last details, Lou asked, "So how much did Nolan say you'd be making as informant?"

"Not a damn penny. He told me that I wouldn't be going to prison is all. You mean I can get some cash for this?"

Lou smiled. "Not anymore, but you should've held out for a better deal."

# CHAPTER 23

*K*aren's eyes popped wide open. Buzzing vibrated up and down her leg. She reached into her pocket and pulled out her phone. She looked at the caller ID. It was blurry. She shook her head and rubbed her eyes, trying to wake herself up. It was Nolan. She hit the red button, and it went straight to voicemail. She collapsed back onto her pillow. Christy was still asleep on the floor. Karen lay on her side and studied the cuts and bruises on her face. This was the second time that Cory assaulted her. The first time he didn't punch and kick her, but he raped her. Christy didn't think it was rape, but how she described the attack and the way Cory forced himself inside of her, there was no doubt in Karen's mind that it was rape. That was three years ago. Karen didn't even know her then. Karen thanked God that Christy began to see the light on what a scumbag her boyfriend really was.

The bruising on her face and neck was more noticeable than it was the night before. The gash over her eye needed a couple of stitches, but the emotional damage Christy sustained far outweighed the physical. Christy and Cory had been together since they were six years old. He was her best friend. They chased butterflies together. Christy told Karen all of it changed when Juice came into the picture. That's why Karen couldn't wrap her head around why Nolan and Juice were spending so much time together.

Karen pulled her covers over her and closed her eyes. Her phone buzzed again. She took it out of her pocket and threw it out the door.

"Who was that?" Karen heard a soft whisper.

"I'm sure it was Nolan trying to apologize for last night at the dance."

Christy rubbed her eyes. "Why would he need to apologize? He had my back when I needed him the most."

Karen sat up to the edge of her bed. "Yeah, but he took off with Juice. He left me and the limo driver to get you home. It took us fifteen minutes to get home and another twenty to wake my dad up and get you to a hospital. And where was Nolan? Off playing grab-ass with his new best friend."

Christy stood up and slid onto the bed next to Karen. "Or he could've been out trying to find Cory. Who knows where to find Cory better than Juice? The two of them at one point were inseparable."

"Yeah, and then Nolan came along. I don't know what it is about him, but he's thrown a major monkey wrench into my life. One minute he can be sweet as pie, and all of his attention is towards me. The next he'll be Juice's lap dog. He follows him everywhere he goes. Sometimes

Juice doesn't even know he's following him. It's kind of pathetic on Nolan's part, if you ask me."

Christy giggled.

"What's so funny?" Karen asked.

"You realize this is the same boy that, as of yesterday, was your dream man. You couldn't stop gushing over him. And now he's Juice's lap dog? I think you're starting to fall hard for this boy. I've never seen you overanalyze every little detail like this. Even when Juice would cheat on you, you let it slide off your back."

Karen buried her head into her pillow so Christy wouldn't see it turn red. Christy got next to her and put her head on the pillow next to Karen. "Do you want to know what's really funny?"

Karen looked over from the pillow. "What?"

"I got beat up by Cory last night, and I'm the one comforting you."

Karen eyes welled up as she wiped away her tears. "I'm sorry. You shouldn't have to deal with my drama. Let's talk about you. Anything you want to get off your chest? I'm all ears."

"Don't cry. I was joking. I don't want to relive the horror of last night."

They heard a knock on the front door. Karen peeked out the window from her bedroom. Nolan was standing there with a box full of chocolates and practicing his apology. Christy nudged Karen to go to the door, but Karen wouldn't go.

Christy stepped in front of Karen and flung open the window. "She's upstairs; come on in. The door's open." Karen looked at her ratty pajama pants she had on and stormed to the bathroom.

Nolan knocked on the bedroom door. "Can I come in?"

Christy stuck her head out the door. "She's just freshening up a bit. Why don't you wait downstairs with Coach Porter? I'm sure he would love to talk."

"I would rather jam an icepick in my eye," Nolan said.

Christy opened the door and gestured with her hand for him to come in. They both stood there. The two of them would make eye contact and quickly turn away. Before last night, they would've been at each other's throats making fun of one another. But Christy couldn't bring herself to poking fun of the man who saved her.

Christy turned to Nolan and asked, "How much does a polar bear weigh?"

"What?"

"How much does a polar bear weigh?"

"I don't know. How much?"

"Enough to break the ice."

Nolan glared in her direction. The blank stare coming from his eyes was enough to make Christy sit down. A few minutes passed, and Nolan laughed quietly and murmured. "Enough to break the ice."

Christy jumped to her feet. "See, I knew that was funny. Your ego is too big to admit it."

"So we're back to taking potshots? If that's the case, I've got a million things I want to get off of my chest."

"Go for it. Anything is better than you sitting there in silence like the creeper from the mall."

"Who's the creeper from the mall?"

"You know the guy. He's always sitting on the benches in the middle of the mall, perving on the young high school girls."

"I don't know who you're talking about, but he can't be much worse than choosing 'Sexy Rexxy' for a Homecoming date."

Christy's cheeks turned rosy. "I thought he would be a tough guy to have around if Cory tried to start anything. The one fatal flaw in my plan was that I left Rex. He could've stepped in to stop him."

Nolan insides wretched, and he turned pale. Should he tell her it was all a setup by Cory? That Rex only took her to Homecoming so that Cory could get her alone. Christy had already gone through hell and back from the night before, so he didn't have the heart to tell her. He also wanted her to stay clear of Cory and Rex. Cory was a ticking time bomb that had already shown violence toward her, and Rex was a follower, plain and simple. If Cory told him to jump into traffic, Rex would find the nearest interstate. He would have no problem roughing up Christy if that's what Cory wanted.

"Christy, I know I sometimes kid around and do things to get under your skin. This time you have to listen to me. Stay away from Cory. No matter how much he says he's sorry, or how many presents he buys you, he's a dangerous guy. I don't mean just beating you up at a school dance dangerous. I mean a legit, criminal, violent danger. And don't rely on Rex to keep you safe. He's going to do whatever Cory tells him. He's a big strong ox who's going to wreck his life as long as he sticks with Cory."

Karen came out of the bathroom with her dark hair pulled back in a ponytail. Nolan couldn't take his eyes off her when her hair was pulled back. Nolan handed her the box of chocolates and kissed her on the cheek.

"Why did you say those things about Cory and Rex?" Karen asked.

"Trust me. Juice and I went after Cory when we found out what he did to Karen. When we finally found him, he was all sorts of crazy. He put a gun to my face and started talking about how he and Juice needed to stick together."

Christy put her hands on top of her head. "What did Juice say to him?"

"He basically said that once he put his hands on you that he didn't want any part of him. Juice has a good heart. I truly believe that. His mom and stepdad both have good jobs. He lives in a nice house, he has a soft spot for the people he cares about, and he's just a little mixed up right now."

Karen tossed the candy onto her bed. "He's more than a little mixed up. I know that he's a drug dealer. When he first started, he would take me to his deals and make me wait in the car. Then he would cheat on me with those "little miss perfects" he would sell weed to. I have no idea why you even mess around with him. One minute you want to fight him, and the next you're defending him. I can't tell what you really think of him."

"He's someone who I need to be friends with at this particular stage in my life. He's someone who let a personal vendetta with your dad take him down a road he should've never gone down. If he was still playing football for your dad, the two of you would still be dating, and I would've never entered the picture."

"That's totally not true." Karen stormed back into the bathroom and slammed the door so hard that the pictures on the wall rattled.

Nolan sighed and began to leave. Christy grabbed him by the arm. "Just so you know, the way she talks about you is something special. I dated Cory for twelve years, and I never talked about him the way she talks about you. So take some unsolicited advice. Swallow your pride. Go tell her you're sorry for being a butt, and take her out to the movies. She wants to go see the new rom-com."

Nolan nodded. "It's not like I don't like her. I think she's the greatest person I've ever met. We might have bad timing. There something that I need to take care of, and that's the only thing I can concentrate on."

Karen came back out of the bathroom. "If I'm the greatest person you've ever met, then take me to the movies tonight."

"Alright, let's go to the damn movies. I would love to take you to see the new chick flick."

"There's a 10:25 p.m. showing tonight," Karen said

"I'm thinking the matinee sounds better. That way we can get ice cream after."

"I'm cool with going to the afternoon showing. I swear I only see you in the daytime. You must have a double life or something."

Nolan laughed. "I do. I have to take care of my grandpa at night. He doesn't get around very well anymore. I'll see you in a few hours."

Nolan left. Then he called Juice and left a message: "Meet me at my house around seven o'clock. Tonight we plant the seed that takes Cory out for good."

# CHAPTER 24

Nolan and Juice met up at the parking lot of the school. Nolan wasn't sure what his plan was going to be, but he always worked better when everything went to hell anyways. They were in a small lot where the administration got to park their cars; only a small patch of well-maintained grass separated the lot from the front door.

Juice got into Nolan's car and lit up a cigarette. "No wonder Bitton's ass is so porky. He only has to walk ten feet a day."

Nolan snatched the cigarette and put it out on the bottom of his shoes. "You're not going to smoke in my car. If you want to give yourself cancer, that's fine, but I'm not going to inhale your smoke."

"You need to chill. We got a long drive ahead of us."

Nolan tilted his head away from Juice. "Where are we going?"

"Mesquite, Nevada," Juice said with a cheesy smile on his face.

Nolan shook his head. "We're not going to Mesquite. I don't feel like driving an hour tonight, and I don't have any reason to be in Mesquite."

Juice laid his seat back all the way and put his hands behind his head. "My boy told me that most of Cory's connections come from Mesquite, so if you want to have a chance at busting him, you need to get your boney ass down to Mesquite."

Nolan rolled down the window and gazed off into the red mountains of Southern Utah. That's what he loved most about St. George. There wasn't anything like those mountains anywhere else in Utah. When he was little, his mom would take him out looking for arrowheadsand other artifacts. His mom always wanted to find a dinosaur bone. Many bones had been discovered right there in their small city. There was too much history for him to sit back and let Cory invade it with drugs.

"Even if we get enough evidence to bust Cory, I have no jurisdiction in Mesquite. We would have to hand him over to the locals."

Juice, still lying in the passenger seat, popped his head up a little. "If you really want to bust Cory, we got to head down there. If you can't figure out how to trace him back to Utah, then you may want to find a new job."

Nolan rubbed his temples with his two index fingers. "Where would we start down there? I don't want to drive down there and have our thumbs up our asses. I can do that from here."

Juice put his seat back up. "I know these two potheads down there who Cory could always count on to get a sale. One of them is always hanging out at a local casino down there, and the other one isn't far behind him. They are always trying to run some scam on the out-of-town rich suits that come in."

Nolan nodded his head and put the car into drive. "Let's go to Mesquite."

They drove through the strip to the outskirts of Mesquite. Nolan turned into a dirt parking lot. He got out of the car and shook his head.

"The Ice Casino, huh?" Nolan asked.

The building was white and brown. Half the shingles on the roof were missing, the paint on the exterior was peeling off, the windows had bars on them, and the parking lot was more weeds than dirt. When they walked inside, Nolan couldn't believe it was even worse than the outside. The shag carpeting hadn't seen a vacuum for a long time, the craps tables were missing dice, the roulette wheel didn't spin, and there wasn't anywhere for a poker game.

Nolan looked at Juice. "You said rich business men come down here. Why on earth would they come to this dump when Vegas is less than an hour away?"

"It's not the gambling they're coming for." Juice pointed to a staircase and went up the stairs. Nolan slowly followed behind him.

When they arrived at the top of the stairs, there was a solid oak door blocking the upstairs from the rest of the building. Juice knocked on it three times very hard. The door unlocked, and a man, who looked like he could bench press a car, opened the door.

"What do you want?"

"Go get Rob," Juice said.

"He's busy. No time for kids play."

Juice stepped up into his face. Nolan wasn't sure if Juice was on a suicide mission or was trying to establish dominance. Either way, Nolan took a step back from the two of them. He didn't want to be in the middle of these two bulls when they collided. Juice poked the man on the chest twice. At this point, Nolan was convinced that Juice was trying to get out of being an informant by getting himself killed.

"Tell him Juice is here to see him."

The man nodded his head and shut the door.

Juice turned toward Nolan and winked. "Can you believe that big gorilla trying to keep me out? Stupid punk looking like some kind of motorcycle gang wannabe. I'll slap his face next time he talks to me like that."

Nolan grabbed a tissue from his pants pocket and wiped the sweat off his forehead. "That dude looks like he kills for fun, and you're stepping up to him like you want to throw down? I knew you had guts, but that took some serious balls."

Juice waved his hand as if it was no big deal. "My Uncle Robbie runs this place. That big oaf wasn't about to do anything. If he did, he wouldn't be employed very long."

The door opened wide. A medium-build man with a silk white shirt, an awesome Yankee pinstripe suit, and a black goatee stood in the door frame. "Is that my nephew, Juicy Juice? Get your ass in here and give me some love, man."

Juice stepped inside and gave his uncle a hug. The two of them talked about his family for a little bit and how he was doing in school. For some strange reason, a man who ran the world's worst casino was pounding it in Juice's head how important school was.

Juice pointed over towards Nolan. "That's my new muscle."

"Man, what happened to Cory. I liked that kid. He had a lot of potential to be my doorman when he graduated," Rob said.

"My new guy beat the hell out of Cory, so I made him my new muscle. Adapt or die, right Uncle Rob?"

"Look at my nephew, always one step ahead of the game. What can I do for you, Juicy?"

"Can we step into your office, Uncle? I have a few things I want to run by you."

Uncle Rob stepped to the side and put his arms out welcoming them in. Nolan followed Juice in. When he stepped through the door, his jaw almost hit the floor. Marble counters on the fully loaded bar, Italian leather couches, hardwood floors, and ten to twelve of the most beautiful women he'd ever laid eyes on.

Nolan tapped Juice on the shoulder. Juice stopped and looked over his shoulder at Nolan, who whispered, "Is your uncle a pimp?"

"No, man. He ain't no purple-suit-wearing, small-time street pimp. He runs a high-class escort service. He doesn't even take money from the women for their dates. He simply charges them rent for the rooms they occupy."

Nolan saw another staircase leading downstairs. He was sure that led to more bedrooms. It was probably blocked off on the lower level so nobody could see the nice part of the building.

Rob opened the door for Nolan and Juice to his office. Surprisingly it was just that. There wasn't anything fancy or extravagant about it. There was a desk with a computer on it, a couple of office chairs, three file cabinets, and a lot of paperwork piled up in his wire "to do" basket.

Rob sat down and took his suit coat off. Nolan looked at that coat knowing that it probably cost more than his entire wardrobe. If he would've seen Rob without being introduced to him, he would've thought he was a Wall Street broker or a New York banker. Nolan stared at Rob's shoes. Black leather, polished, and no shoe laces. Nolan had never known a pair of shoes to keep his attention, but these were different altogether.

Rob looked at Nolan and smiled. "You like those shoes, do ya?"

"Yeah, I've never been a shoe guy, but I could see myself owning a pair of those one day."

Rob took the right shoe off and began stroking it. "I had this handcrafted from a man I know in Italy. What size shoe do you wear?"

Nolan glanced down at his New Balance tennis shoes. "These are nine-and-a-half, but I usually wear a ten."

Rob walked over to one of the filing cabinets and opened the bottom drawer. He pulled out a pair of black shoes. "These are one of my older pairs, handcrafted and everything. All you need to do is put a little polish on them, and you'll be styling. Well, at least your feet will be."

He tossed the shoes over to Nolan. "Geez, thanks Rob. I don't know what else to say."

"No worries, man. Those were just rotting away up here." Rob then turned his attention toward Juice. "Juicy, what brings you down here, nephew? Your mom told me if I gave you anymore money, she was going to gut me. And seeing how she could handle my big brother back in the day, I believe she'll make good on that promise."

Juice sat down in one of the chairs and put his feet up on the desk. "I do need something from you, Uncle, but it's not money. It's just a little info."

Rob walked over to where Juice's feet were up and politely put them back on the ground. "If it's information that you need, then I have a wealth of it."

"Does that one tweeker that Cory slings to still hang around here? I know that you used to let him vacuum the downstairs and keep things clean, but from the looks of that hellhole, it looks like you may have canned him."

Rob loosened up his tie and unbuttoned the top button of his shirt. "Do you mean Dennis? I remember when you and Cory first met him. He was downstairs trying to play a game of craps. By some miracle, he kept rolling sevens. That kid cleaned me out that night. I guess you and your drug-dealing buddy saw an opportunity and pounced on the poor kid. I don't know if he left with any of that money he won that night. Cory hooked him up real good."

"That's him. So do you know where he's at?" Juice asked.

"I'm surprised you're coming to me with this question. He came into my office about six weeks ago and thanked me for all the help I'd given him over the years. He told me that Cory had given him a better opportunity to advance in his business."

Juice fell out of his chair. "Cory has a druggie working for him? That dude snorts the shit as fast as he can get his hands on it. Dennis always used to hang out with some other skinny, white, stoner-looking dude. Where is he at?"

"Yeah, I remember him. He always had that stupid hand-knitted beanie on. It's over ninety-five degrees most of the year down here, and that moron is walking around in jeans and a beanie. Last I heard, he's not a good customer anymore. Got his act together and got a valet parking job at one of the nicer casinos."

Nolan, still mesmerized by his new shoes, asked Rob, "Why do you have such a dump of a casino downstairs and a beautiful brothel up here. If you're using it for a front to cover up the sex you're selling, shouldn't the casino be nice?"

Rob stood up and pounded the table. "That Casino isn't a front or anything other than what it is. The escort service is completely legit. We don't sell sex. We sell companionship; and wherever the night leads two adults, then that's their business. They're two separate enterprises run out of the same building. I happen to put more money in the one that made me more money."

Nolan scratched his head. "Escort service is a fancy way of saying whorehouse. You have bedrooms everywhere up here. If you don't want the police to look into this further, then you should at least clean the casino up."

Rob sat back down and took his tie off. "Those beautiful young ladies rent the rooms from me. Most of them aren't even employed by me. I just collect rent at the end of the week."

"End of the week, huh?" Nolan asked.

Juice grabbed one of Nolan's new shoes and hit him in the chest with it. "Why are you asking all of these stupid-ass questions? We got the info we came for from Robbie, and you're going to treat him like dirt?"

Nolan grabbed the shoe back and put it under his arm. "You're right. Rob, I'm sorry. I think that if you cleaned up the casino area a little bit, then you would draw a more positive attention to your place."

Rob smiled. "What makes you think I want any attention at all? Don't worry about it though, my man. I like a guy who isn't afraid to speak his mind."

Juice gave Rob a hug. Rob showed them out, and Juice and Nolan went back to the car. Nolan started up the car and looked over to Juice. "Now what?"

# CHAPTER 25

Juice and Nolan drove into the Salt River Casino parking lot. It was the fourth casino they'd been to that night. They pulled into the valet parking and waited for the attendant. When he approached their car, Juice got out of the passenger seat.

"What's up, my man? We're looking for a skinny, jittery, ex-junkie. From what I can remember, he's around six feet, but he has no meat on his bones. You know anyone like that who works here?"

The attendant opened the driver's side door. "Not anymore. He's long gone."

Nolan noticed an old, hand-knitted beanie in the valet's back pocket. "When's the last time that you saw Dennis?" Nolan asked.

Without thinking, he responded, "I saw him last week at a pickup basketball game by the brickyard."

Juice ran over to the valet and began to inspect him. "You're the stoner that always followed Dennis around."

He sunk his head down low. "What do you want, Juice? I'm in the middle of my shift, and I haven't touched any of that junk for six months. As far as I'm concerned, you and I have no business."

Nolan put his hand out to shake. "I'm Nolan, and you've already given us all that we need. We're going to head down to the Brickyard to try and find out if Dennis has been dealing down there."

The valet shook Nolan's hand. "I'm Duke. Let me give you some advice. Don't hang around a scumbag like Juice. It only leads to unwanted attention from the police, dealers, or whores."

"You don't have to worry about that with Nolan; he's as straight as an arrow." Juice patted Nolan on the back then turned back and stared at Duke. "You look like a totally different man. What the hell you been doing to look halfway normal?"

"Once I decided to get clean, I needed the high I used to get from drugs. I joined a workout program that promotes the natural high as opposed to the artificial. I've been healthy and living right."

Nolan put his arm around Duke's shoulder. "Yep, if it wasn't for that beanie in your back pocket, we would've probably driven right on by to the next casino. If you alert Dennis that we're coming for him, then I'm going to come back and let Juice kick your teeth down your throat."

Duke nodded. "If you're going to look for Dennis, I wouldn't start at the courts on the Brickyard. He'll be working tonight. Try the gym by your uncle's casino."

"Why the gym?" Nolan asked.

"Because he's selling those horse steroids that Cory gives him."

Juice interrupted the conversation. "They got Dennis slinging testosterone? Why not weed or something he might be useful at?"

"Would you give Dennis any drugs? He would smoke or inject it before he sold any of it. Give him steroids and he becomes a pretty reliable drug dealer," Duke said.

Nolan gave Duke a twenty-dollar bill for his time and got back into the car. He honked the horn and waved for Juice to get back in. They peeled out and headed west, back toward the gym.

When they arrived, there was only one car in the lot. It was the dead of the night, so not many people were working out. Nolan went into the gym and asked a few questions while Juice stayed in the car, waiting to see if Dennis showed up. After a few minutes, Nolan returned and turned the car off.

"He'll be here, the front desk guy thinks," Nolan said.

Juice rolled down his window to let the crisp air hit his face. "What did he say?"

"He said that the only guy in there lifting is his best customer. They meet around closing time, which is 1:00 a.m. We have to sit and wait it out."

Juice opened the car door and took off his baggy sweater. He had a plain white T-shirt on underneath his sweater and gym shorts. He tightened his shoelaces up and looked at Nolan. "I'm not going to sit here and wait. I'm going to go get my lift in for the night."

Nolan waited for two hours for Juice to be finished with his workout. He listened to music, played with his cell phone, and kept his eye out for Dennis. Nolan didn't like stakeouts. It gave him time to think, and being alone with his thoughts made him shiver. He would daydream about his mom dying on the job a lot. He'd wonder where his dad went and never came back from. He would wonder how Karen would take the news of him being a cop when he had to break his cover. Would she be upset that he lied to her, or would she still date him? Being alone in a car by himself was almost as dangerous to Nolan as getting shot at.

Nolan snapped out of his dreaming long enough to realize Juice was back in the car. Juice stared at Nolan befuddled. "I've been saying your name for the past five minutes. What the hell's going on in that dome of yours?"

Nolan shook his head to clear the cobwebs. "Nothing. Don't worry, I was in the zone. I was imagining where we could go to find Dennis."

"Imagine no more. He'll be here in a couple minutes."

"How do you know that?"

"That bro lifting in the gym told me so. I needed a spot on my squat, so I asked if he'd help me out. I got to talking with him, and he told me he was meeting his steroid guy when he was finished lifting."

Nolan rubbed his forehead with his index finger and thumb. "He told you all this because you asked him?"

"No. It's the bodybuilder brotherhood. We talked about some of the competitions that we've been in and what's the best protein shake. All that stuff that we're interested in. He told me that his guy hooked him up with the best stuff and that I should give it a try. Little does he know, it's the same shit I've been dealing for years. I told him I was interested, and he said his guy was coming."

Nolan sighed. "The bodybuilder brotherhood. I've heard it all."

The weightlifter came out of the gym and waited on the steps. A small guy approached him and began to talk. Nolan jumped out of the car and darted toward them. The man on the stairs hopped to his feet. Nolan grabbed the skinny guy by the back of his neck. "Dennis, I've been looking for you. Why don't you come have a chat with me?"

Dennis yelped like a defenseless puppy. "Who are you? What do you want with me? I've done nothing wrong."

"Besides being a complete tool?" Juice asked.

Dennis turned around, pale as a ghost. His voice began to squeak even higher. "What is Juice doing here? Are you guys here to kill me? Please Juice, don't hurt me. Cory and I have an understanding. Don't do this."

Nolan let go of Dennis. "Nobody is here to kill you, Dennis." Nolan heard some commotion behind him and turned around. Juice stood over the body of a knocked out bodybuilder.

"What did you do that for?"

Juice shook his hand back and forth. "He was bum-rushing you when you grabbed Dennis, so I cold-cocked him."

"Thanks, I guess. Let's try to keep the assaults to a minimum though?"

Juice nodded his head. "You're the boss."

Nolan turned his attention back to Dennis. "What kind of agreement do you have with Cory?"

Dennis shook like a leaf and muttered something. Nolan couldn't understand what he said. Nolan grabbed him by both his shoulders. "Dennis, you need to calm down. I'm not going to hurt you. I won't let Juice hurt you. I need to know what your arrangement with Cory is."

Dennis took three deep breaths and began speaking softly. Nolan had to lean his ear right next to his mouth just hear him. "I owe Cory a lot of money. He's letting me work it off. I find people to sell horse pills to, and he'll cover my debt. I've sold way more than I owe though. That's why I thought you were coming to kill me."

"Dennis, you need to be completely truthful with me right now. When are you meeting Cory again?"

"Tonight; I'm going to give him the money from tonight's sales. We're meeting at the courts."

Nolan brushed Dennis' clothes off from where he had a grasp of him. "The Brickyard courts?"

"I pull up right on the blacktop and unroll my window. I don't even have to get out of my car. He comes out from behind the rock wall. I give him the money, and he gives me some crumbs to live on until next week."

"Why don't you keep all of that money tonight? You won't be needed tonight on the courts. Let us handle it."

Dennis gladly put the money in his pocket and faded away into the night. Nolan got back in the car, pulled out his phone, and dialed Lou's number. Lou answered on the other line. "I have good news," Nolan said. "I know where Cory is going to be with a lot of drugs tonight."

There was a moment of silence on the line. "That would be good news, Nolan, if Cory wasn't lying face down in a cheap motel here in St George."

"He's dead? What happened?"

"Someone shot him in the back of the head."

"What motel? I'm on my way there."

"No! You're still undercover, and now you're not looking for a local dealer, you're looking for a murderer."

Nolan hung up the phone and looked over at Juice. "Cory's dead. We need to find a new way to the top of the drug chain."

Driving back from Mesquite at 1:00 a.m. in complete silence gave Nolan a lot of time to let his mind wander. *Who would want to murder a small-time nickel-and-dime drug dealer. Was it a drug deal gone wrong, or something very different? Why a cheap motel? Most of Cory's drug deals were in public places.*

Nolan and Juice cruised up the I-15 until they came to the St. George exit. Nolan turned down the small cul-de-sac toward Juice's house. When he arrived at Juice's house, Juice opened the door and got out without either of them saying a word. Nolan drove around a little longer and circled the Vard a few times. Then he turned down Skyline Drive toward the motels. He knew he wasn't supposed to go to the crime scene, but he wouldn't be able to sleep tonight if he didn't at least drive by the scene. He crept slowly past the Elk Ridge Motel and peeked out his driver-side window. The crowd blocked his view. Nolan parked a block away from the motel and meandered over toward the scene. He pulled his hoodie over his head and looked at the ground, trying to blend in with the rest of the bystanders. He muddled his way in between a few people behind the yellow tape.

Standing on his toes and straining his neck, he couldn't get a glimpse of Cory's body. He managed to finagle his way to the front of the crowd. He reached into his front jeans pockets and pulled out a little pair of binoculars. When he looked through them, he felt his head whiplashed from something pulling him in the opposite direction. He freed himself from the iron-tight clamp and spun around.

Grandpa Jared towered over him with steam coming from his ears. "Nolan, you need to get out of here."

"What are you doing here, Grandpa? Shouldn't you be in bed or watching an old episode of *Cops*?"

"Don't worry about what I'm doing here. What the hell are you doing here? If you want to be employed in the morning, then I would suggest you get back to the house. I'll fill you in on the details when I get home."

Nolan shrugged his shoulder. "Nobody knows what I'm doing here. I did a pretty good job of making it look like I was another gawker staring at a murder. We get like two deaths a year, so it's not out of the ordinary that there's a crowd gathered around."

"You're right, Nolan. It's not strange that people are gathered around trying to get a glimpse at what's going on, but your commanding officer told you to stay away. Disobeying a direct order from Lou is career suicide. Also, you didn't do as great of a job as you think you did about blending in with the crowd. You had your binoculars in hand staring at the scene. What civilian would carry police-issued binoculars? You stood out like a sore thumb. Get your skinny butt back to the house. I'll fill you in later."

Nolan stomped away, back to the car. Whenever he got mad, he would mumble inaudibly to himself and get himself more worked up. By the time he got to his car and drove home, he was ready to rip a bear, limb from limb. He paced back and forth throughout the entire house.

He finally sat down and sent a text out to Karen. "Did you hear that Cory died tonight?"

He put his feet up on the ottoman and waited for her response. He heard his phone ding, and he looked at it. "Yeah, it's all over Twitter already. They say he was murdered. That's scary that something like that could happen."

"From what I've known of Cory, he hung out with some shady characters. It's not surprising that he would end up dead in a motel."

"Cory and you both hang out with Juice!!!! How long until you're murdered?"

Nolan read the message and laughed. She did have a point, but Nolan considered his training to be the great equalizer. He wasn't going to end up dead by the likes of some street thug trying to get a fix. He put his phone on silent and went to sleep.

The next morning he woke up to Jared and a deep voice talking in the kitchen. Nolan got up and felt a sting in his neck. Sleeping on a love seat and footstool must have given him a pinched nerve. He stretched his neck out and went into the kitchen.

He strolled in and saw Lou and his grandpa sitting at the counter. Each of them had a cup of coffee, and there were files and pictures spread all over the table and counter. Nolan pulled a soda out of the refrigerator and cracked it open.

Lou leaned back in his chair. "How do you drink that crap in the morning? It's pure sugar and caffeine."

Nolan picked up the empty sugar container on the kitchen counter and shook it. "Don't lecture me about how much sugar I have in a soda when this container was halfway full yesterday. Exactly how much did you use in your coffee this morning?"

Lou gave a hardy chuckle. "Touché."

Nolan sat down by them. They looked around at each other for a few minutes. Nobody wanted to break the ice. They all finished their drinks. Lou got up and put his coffee mug in the sink. With his back turned to then, Lou blurted out, "You disobeyed a direct order. What if someone would've put two-and-two together?"

"How would they do that, Lou? I was just another gawker staring at the murder of a young kid."

Nolan's grandpa slammed his fist on the counter with so much force that his coffee mug flew off. "You don't always have to go against the grain with us. Lou's been at this for thirty-one years, and I retired with forty-three years under my belt. The only way you're going to make it as an undercover or a uni, for that matter, is for you to listen and learn. When Lou tells you to stay away from the scene, you damn well better stay away!"

Nolan sunk his head like a scolded puppy after peeing on the rug. Lou sat back down at the table and spoke softly. "I guess nobody made you, so no harm no foul."

Nolan nodded his head. "What can you tell me about Cory's death?"

Lou scratched his chin, scanning for the details that he could remember. "Stabbed three times in the chest. One of them punctured his heart, and he bled out. He had a lot of cash on him at the time. He had over three thousand dollars, but no drugs. My best guess was he was there dealing at the hotel. I don't think it was a drug deal gone badly though. Any druggie would've taken the money and drugs had they killed him."

Nolan leaned in. "What's your theory then?"

"I don't really have one. We have some things to go on since you've gotten to know him the last few weeks, but we're going to have to interview people that knew him, try and find out which junkie he met in that hotel room. We've got forensics working on it, but in a dump like that, there's going to be a lot of DNA from a lot of weeks. I felt like I needed a shower after I left last night."

"Juice is going to be our biggest asset. He knows Cory's clients. He knows where he likes to deal out of, and he was his best friend," Nolan said.

"I thought you replaced him?" Nolan's Grandpa asked.

"Cory and Juice were like brothers, even if they were fighting a little bit. Juice is going to sing like a bird in order to catch Cory's killer."

"I still don't trust that punk," Lou said.

"I don't really trust him either, but so far since he's been on with me, he's been a model citizen. I'm not saying that he's going to lead me to the kingpin, but he helped me track Cory's deals down in Mesquite. I'm fairly certain that he knew Cory was going to wind up dead or in prison, so he was doing everything in his power to save him. Now that he's been murdered, Juice is going to be all hands on deck. Juice may be a tough high schooler, but he's doesn't want to end up dead."

Lou leaned his elbows on the table. "We'll figure out who killed Cory. It's only a matter of time. With Juice's help, we can nail this thing down quickly. My biggest concern is who to focus on with the drugs at Red Rock? With Cory dead and Juice as an informant, that ties our hands pretty good."

Nolan closed his eyes and leaned back on his chair, remembering every detail that'd happened for the last six weeks. "We know that Ken is our only other option at this point, but Ken is smart. The minute I met Cory and Juice, I knew they were into some shady dealings. However, when Ken showed up at Juice's house that night, he could've pushed me over with one finger. Some of the other lifters in Juice's crew are on steroids, but I'm not sure if any of them are dealing. When Cory and I got into that fight, things changed. He didn't like or respect me, but there was an understanding that I wouldn't be pushed around. If I do that to Ken, he will shut me out, and we'll lose any and all contact."

"You've already exchanged drugs and money with Ken. Why don't you make the arrest?" Jared said.

Nolan shook his head. "I haven't been undercover for very long. I can get more intel on Ken, and the charges will stick. Besides Ken is small time. If we arrest him, someone will take his spot before the end of the day, and Red Rock High will be in the same situation in two weeks. We can shoot for the moon on this one. It already spans two states."

Lou looked Nolan dead in the eyes. "Sometimes making the easy arrest is the right arrest. I'll always back my agent in the field, but I need to know that your intentions aren't selfish. I need to know you're not going for the kingpin for your own career advancement. If taking Ken out of the school will make it safer, then we need to do that."

Nolan pleaded with Lou. "It won't make it safer. It could potentially make it more dangerous. Who knows who would replace Ken if we arrest him? Ken may be a drug dealer, but he's not going to go rogue and start hurting people. Let's work the Ken angle and the Cory murder. Let me kill two birds with one stone."

Lou nodded his head. "I'm going to do some interviews with the students at the school about Cory. I need to get a better gauge on the type of kid he was. We'll be in the school. We're going to pull you in as well. Everyone knows you and Cory didn't get along. When we pull you in, we're going to interview you just like everyone else. You'll be full-blown undercover still. You need to make sure Juice is, as well."

Lou and Jared stood up from the counter and went to the front door. They talked about something for a couple of minutes, probably on how to control Nolan. Lou left and Jared went upstairs.

Nolan sat at the table for a couple of minutes. He noticed he'd missed a text from Karen: "Who do you think killed Cory?"

# CHAPTER 26

*T*he next week at school was a blur for all involved. Nolan had to shake his head at some of the rumors coming out about Cory's death. He heard that Christy had a hit man hired to kill Cory after what he did to her at Homecoming. Another great rumor was that Cory shot himself in the back of the head over losing Christy. Nolan's personal favorite was that Juice did it in a fit of roid rage after their workout together. The most popular one that gained traction within the school was that Nolan killed him to prove to Juice that he could do what it took to be the new man in town. Nolan knew that students believed it by the weird way they looked at him, or they would run to the other side of the hallway when he walked past them.

All the rumors made for fun stories, but the reality was that nobody knew what happened to Cory that night. The facts of the case, as Lou relayed them, were that Cory met with someone at the motel, the medical examiner found cuts and bruises on his knuckles—so Cory fought his killer—and he had a wad of cash on him.

Lou and his squad had been at the school asking general questions, but they came to the very quick conclusion that nobody in the school had anything to do with the murder. Nolan felt the weight of the world come off his chest when Lou told him that. It was going to be nearly impossible to get Ken to trust him. But not having a murderer on the loose in the halls made Nolan's job easier.

Lou and Bitton still had a counselor at the school in case anyone wanted to talk about how Cory's death affected them, but not many students went to talk to him. Cory had Juice as a best friend and a couple of stooges, but no one was heartbroken over his death. That was sadder than the actual death. Christy talked to the counselor and had nothing but great things to say about him. Christy may have hated the son of a bitch, but there is a really thin line between love and hate.

Nolan was throwing licked gummy bears at his math teacher's ceiling, trying to get them to stick, when an office aide came in and handed him a note. It read that the grievance counselor wanted to talk to him. He got up from his chair and headed down to the counselor's room. Nolan paused before he knocked on the office door. His mind raced about what he could possibly want? Did he know who Nolan really was, or did he hear the rumors about Cory and him? Nolan knocked quietly and waited.

A loud booming voice echoed through the solid oak door. "Come in."

Nolan entered. He saw the counselor and sighed. He then cracked up laughing.

"You're the crisis counselor, Grandpa?"

"Yeah, Lou thought it would be a good idea if I could get some clues out of the grieving kids. I thought Cory was popular though. I've only had two or three kids come in and talk."

Nolan leaned up against the wall and folded his arms. "You realize we're going to hell for this one. He sent you in to interrogate kids and they don't even realize it. They think you're some kind of grievance expert."

"Did you not notice my degrees on the wall at home? I've got my PhD in Psychology from the University of Utah. I'm more than qualified to help kids out. If I get some valuable information along the way, then I'll be more than happy to share it."

"Don't you think this will compromise my cover with you being here?"

"No. I told everyone I'm your grandfather and that you live with me. As far as they know, Principal Bitton hired me as an outside source to help the process." Jared sat back in is big desk chair and leaned all the way back.

"I see that you're comfy. Has anyone given you any valuable information, Doctor?" Nolan asked.

"Not on my end. Mostly Christy telling me how she wanted to feel bad about Cory's death, but she couldn't muster up any sorrow. She felt guilty for not feeling pain, but she didn't feel the actual pain that she thought she should be feeling. After some of the horrific details she shared with me about Cory, I can't blame her one bit for not feeling any pain. Did you know the first time they slept together it was rape? She begged him to stop, but he just told her he wasn't going to stop until he finished.

She started the diesel engine, but only he could turn it off."

Nolan sat down. He clenched his hands and felt the heat rising to his face. "Whoever killed Cory did the world a favor, as far as I'm concerned. Why are we even looking for his murderer? We should be buying him a round of shots."

Jared furrowed his brow and shook his head. "That's not how being a cop works, Nolan. You can't pick and choose who you want to go after. Even if the person who killed Cory was a saint and donated all of his money to feed starving children, he still needs to be prosecuted. We don't investigate only when good guys are killed. For heaven's sake, if we didn't investigate low-life scumbags who were killed, we wouldn't have more than one case a decade. The fact of the matter is that shady people solicit other shady people. Should we not investigate a drive-by shooting because both shooter and victim were in a gang? Of course not. It's our job to make the streets safe."

"I get that, Grandpa, but this one is personal. He physically abused Christy, he damn near broke my esophagus when he threw that bottle at me, and he's a pretty big drug dealer. You add all these things together, and I think the street's a lot safer tonight without Cory."

Jared threw his arms in the air. "Yeah sure, you make a compelling argument. Maybe I'll just let the evidence go down the toilet because Cory beat up a woman."

"You have evidence?" Nolan stood up and ran around the desk shoulder-to-shoulder with Jared.

Jared held his hand out and nudged Nolan away from him. "Don't piss yourself from excitement. It's not much, but it's a start."

Nolan grabbed one of the office chairs and pulled it up next to his grandpa's. "Tell me."

Jared rolled his chair away from Nolan toward the back of the room. Jared had a touch of claustrophobia, and when Nolan got excited like this, he only added to it. "It was a long, blonde hair. One of the unis found it under his sweater. We sent it to the lab to see if we could get a hit on it. Sure enough, it came back to Crystal Sweetney."

"Who the hell is Crystal Sweetney?"

"She's some hooker out of Nevada. She'd been picked up a couple of times in Utah for prostitution, but I guess she decided to go where the laws weren't too strict on prostitution. We got the Vegas PD running down last-known address and employment, but we haven't heard back. She used to work out of this dump in Mesquite, but no one has seen her there for a while."

Nolan jumped out of his chair. "Was it the Ice Casino in Mesquite?"

"Yeah, how did you know that?"

"Juice's Uncle Rob owns that spot. He gave me the new shoes I've been wearing around for the past week. Rob's a good guy."

Jared rolled his chair back to his desk. "Don't go investigating this on your own. Let me take this to Lou before you do anything?"

"What's Lou going to do? Robbie won't talk to the cops. He's too smart for that. If he knows where Crystal is, he'll tell me and Juice way before you get a sniff of her."

"I'll run it past Lou." Jared clinched his jaw tight. "But your main focus is Ken and the drugs he's peddling out to this school. Let Lou and the other detectives handle the murder. If he can use you, he will."

Nolan got up to leave. "Yeah, I got it. Go after Ken, get the drugs."

"I'm serious." Jared slammed a drawer shut on his desk. "Don't do anything that will make me have to kick your ass. Drugs . . . go find the drugs."

Nolan whizzed out the door. He heard Jared say something, but it didn't register with him. He jumped like a rabbit through the hallways looking for Juice. He would pop his head into all of the spots that Juice liked to hang out by in school. The weight room, the lunchroom, by Karen's locker . . . but he was nowhere to be found.

He asked anyone he passed in the hallway if they'd seen Juice. Nobody had. He went outside to look around. Maybe he had come out for a smoke, or maybe he and Ken were planning their next deal. Still, Juice was missing.

Sitting on the stairs that led to the lunchroom, Nolan began to think. *What if he already knows his uncle's escorts were there? What if the person who murdered Cory came looking for Juice?* The school bell rang, and the lunchroom began to fill up. Nolan went to the table that Juice and his team usually sat at and waited. A couple of the lifters sat down with their homemade rice and chicken and shoveled it in their mouths. Juice had taught this group that food isn't for taste but, rather, for fuel. They all bought it, hook, line, and sinker. These kids listened to Juice like he was an answer to their prayers. But in reality, Juice liked a good double cheeseburger as much as anyone.

Nolan felt a slap on his back. It was Juice. "What's happening, big Noles?"

Nolan pounded the lunch table. "Where have you been? I looked through the entire school and outside of it."

"You must not have looked too hard because I was in the auto shop."

"You were in class? You never go to class. What were you doing there? Trying to figure out a way to hollow out some more secret compartments in Ken's truck?"

"This thing with Cory . . ." Juice fought hard to keep his voice from cracking. "This thing with Cory's got me thinking that I need to get to class."

Nolan grabbed one of the kid's water bottles at the table and opened it. He took a drink of it and handed it back to the kid. "I get where you're coming from, but we need to get after it now, more than ever."

Juice pulled out a chocolate bar and took a bite. Half the kids at the table gasped and couldn't believe Juice was eating candy. "It's dark chocolate," he snapped at them. He turned to Nolan. "I hear what you're saying, but we're going to have to figure out how I can go to class and do our thing."

"Since when did school become so important to you? I'm having a hard time wrapping my mind around why all of a sudden you can't skip a class or two."

"You may not be as good as you think you are if you can't figure that one out." Juice took another bite of the candy bar. "I want to help you out; but when that's over, where does that leave me? I need a high school diploma to join the police academy."

Nolan fell out of his chair. "If you're not Juice or me, get out of here right now." The kids stood up and scrammed like cockroaches. "Since when do you want to be a cop? You're a damn drug dealer."

"I'm giving that shit up. I've never been caught, and I never will. No more selling for me." Juice finished his candy bar and placed the wrapper in Nolan's front shirt pocket.

"You can't get out. We need to catch Ken and his supplier. When that happens, then you can go chase your tail at the academy. Plus, I got a lead on who killed Cory. He wasn't at the motel for a drug deal, he was there for sex."

"Sex? Who was he doing that with, and how would you know that?" Juice asked.

"We found a hair that belonged to one of your uncle's escorts. We find her, we solve the case, I put in a good word for you at the academy, and everyone's happy."

"I don't know." Juice put his head down on the table. "Why don't you let the others take care of the murder. We'll catch Ken."

"I can't do that." Nolan stood up and walked away. "There's more fame in catching a murder."

# CHAPTER 27

*J*ared sat in his school-issued temporary office, stretching his arms overhead and yawning, when his door flung open and Juice came sprinting in. He bent over at the waist, hands on his knees, trying to catch his breath. "Nolan's going to do something stupid."

"What?" Jared pulled up a chair for Juice to catch his breath. "What's he going to do?"

Juice took a couple of deep breaths. "He's going to see my Uncle Rob." Juice grabbed water out of his backpack and took a long drink. "Nolan thinks that he and Rob are on the up and up, but they're not."

"Why does he think that he and Rob are friends?"

"I took him down there when we were trying to find out about Cory's drug deals. I introduced them, Rob gave him some shoes, and everything went off without a hitch. What he doesn't know is that I called ahead and told him to be on his best behavior. I told him I had some company with me, the kind that could put them silver bracelets on."

Jared opened his desk drawer and pulled out his old Colt .45 Peacemaker. He spun the chamber around a few times and checked the ammo. "You told your uncle that Nolan was a cop? You slimy little bastard. You know if anything happens to him, I'm putting this gun to your head and pulling the trigger."

"I had to tell him." Juice squirmed in his chair. "If Rob would've found out I brought a cop to his joint and didn't tell him, both of us would've ended up six feet under."

"How would he have found out? The only possible way that he could've found out is if you had told him. "

"No sir. Uncle Rob is connected in more ways than you could imagine. He would've found out. I know he knows who killed Cory. Rob has his finger on the pulse of everything. That's why we have to get Nolan out of there."

Jared calmly stroked his silver mustache. "How long ago did he leave?"

"About five minutes. As soon as he told me he wanted to go talk to Rob, I came here to tell you."

"You call your uncle and tell him that Nolan's trying to come down. I'm going to call Lou and have one of the black-and-whites pick him up before he crosses the state line."

Juice and Jared made their phone calls and raced out to the parking lot. They jumped in Jared's old Chevy pickup and headed south toward Nevada. As soon as they got on to the freeway, Jared's phone rang. "Hello." Jared nodded his head. "Oh good, I'll see you there. Thank you; I owe you one."

He hung up the phone and took the next available exit. "A couple of the units stopped Nolan before he got out of town. He's back at the precinct."

Jared got a big smile on his face and sang to the radio. Juice put his fingers in his ears. "What's the matter, you don't like Chris Ledoux?" Jared asked.

"Not my style. I'm more into rap or old-school hip hop. I don't dig on this hilly-billy stuff."

"You know, son, I've been racking my brain on a few things. Why on earth did you agree to be an informant?" Jared asked.

"Nolan said that he was going to throw me in jail if I didn't become his snitch."

"Yeah, he probably could've with the crimes he's witnessed." Jared, still humming along with the beat, continued, "One thing that you have to keep in mind with Nolan . . . You're too small for him. He's always looking for the big one. He hasn't fully grasped the concept of doing your job without recognition."

"Is that what makes a good cop?"

"It's part of it? Why do you ask?"

Juice fidgeted with his seatbelt. "I want to join the police academy when I graduate. Being with Nolan has opened my eyes on what I want to do with my life."

Jared patted Juice's shoulder. "Good for you. You don't have a record, do you? You know you can't join with a police record, right?"

"I've been lucky. I've broken the law, but I haven't been caught."

"You haven't been caught yet. If Nolan wasn't so gung-ho on trying to find the biggest drug lord In Utah, you would've been arrested, and this would all be just a dream."

"Yeah, that's why I want to get out of it, but Nolan said I need to help him out with this case and then he'd help me out getting into the academy. "

"Just because you're our informant doesn't mean you can break the law. If I were you, I would let Nolan become Ken's go-to guy. Help set it up. Tell Ken that you want out, but Nolan will take your spot. All these dealers don't care who sells their drugs as long as their drugs get sold."

Tears rolled down Juice's face. "This is the first time in a long time that someone has looked out for me. My mom and stepdad love me, but all they look out for is their careers."

"Wipe those tears from your eyes. You've still got to prove that you're not all about the drug life."

"I will. How can I do that, sir?"

"The best thing you can do is show Nolan how Ken's operations work. Let Nolan get inside and out of it, that way when you want to leave, Ken will trust Nolan enough to let him take your clientele. That keeps Nolan busy and leaves us with the murder at hand."

"You sure you're Nolan's grandpa? That dude's a "blow a gasket first, think second" type of guy. You're the exact opposite."

The smile quickly ran away from Jared's face, and he gripped the steering wheel tight. "His mom was a react-first type of person. That's why I have to raise him."

# CHAPTER 28

$A$t the station, Nolan sulked and waited for Jared to arrive. Lou pulled him into his office and read him the riot act. Nolan pouted like a new puppy in the corner chair of the office. Catching a murderer had to be the department's first priority, so Nolan couldn't figure out why his ass got chewed. All he wanted to do was bring him to justice.

Lou gave Nolan the choice to wait for Jared out in the cold or in the drunk tank, but Lou didn't want to look at Nolan's face anymore. As soon as Nolan left the office, he snatched his keys out of his pocket and went to the back lot. He jumped in his car and fired it up. He put it in reverse and looked in the rearview mirror. There were two black-and-white units blocking him in. Nolan flung the door open so hard that it bounced back and hit him. The officers blurted out in uncontrollable laughter.

"Get out of my way!" Nolan yelled.

One of the officers sat on the trunk of Nolan's car. "Sorry, man. We have our orders not to let you leave until Jared Dixon gets here."

"Jared's my grandpa. He won't care if I take off."

"It's not going to happen. I'm not going to disobey a direct order from my superior. Last guy who did that ended up getting water-boarded in a dumpy warehouse."

Nolan shrugged his jacket off. "You want to be a funny guy? How about I knock that smile off of your face?"

Jared and Juice screeched into the back lot. Juice sprang from the car and grabbed Nolan in a bear hug. Jared walked calmly around the car. He patted the officer on the shoulder and whispered something into his ear. The officer jumped off the trunk of Nolan's car and shook Jared's hand. He motioned for the other officers to disperse. Jared leaned on the car silently, collecting his thoughts.

"Where do I start Nolan? Did our conversation at the breakfast table mean anything to you? It's time you start falling in line with what the rest of the department is doing."

"That's crap." Nolan leaned down and picked up his jacket and put it back on. "The rest of the department gets to work on the murder of Cory, and I have to play the high school student looking for drugs."

"You wanted undercover work. Do you remember that? You begged Lou to put you out, and I thought it was a bad idea from the get-go."

Nolan punched his car and left a giant dent in the door. "Cory's murder is part of the undercover work. Cory went to the school that I'm investigating. I'm stuck not investigating his murder while everyone else gets a piece of my pie."

"Stop!" Jared walked over, nose to nose with Nolan. "Nobody is getting a piece of your pie. The guys who were blocking you in have worked here a lot longer than you have, and they're still writing parking tickets at the local junior college. There are detectives who have put in the time and work that should be cracking the drug deals in St. George. All you ever see is you getting the shaft, but all anyone else sees is all the opportunities that you get because of me and your mom."

"I don't think my Mom has anything to do with it. In case you forgot, she's dead."

Jared backed away from Nolan. "Do you know how she died? I mean the details of what went down the day I lost my daughter?"

"Of course I do. She was shot in the back while she was walking her beat."

"That's only partially right. The morning of that day, she went in to work just like any other day. I was still the police chief then. She stormed into my office and started making accusations about why she hadn't been made a detective yet. She believed that I held her back because I was too sexist to let a woman become a detective. The truth of the matter was, she wasn't nearly ready. She had only passed the test a month earlier, and she had an itchy trigger finger. She and Lou were actually partners back then. They were patrolling the streets that day when your mother saw a shoplifter running out of a gas station. Lou must've seen the gun in the perp's hand, because he called for backup immediately. Meanwhile, your mom chased after him, leaving Lou in the dust. He screamed out for her to get back in the car, that they could catch him more quickly because he was running down the street. Your mom continued on chasing him, Lou said. Lou jumped in the car and tore down the road. When he caught up to your mom, she was already shot, lying on the ground dying. The guy hid behind a dumpster around the corner and killed her in cold blood. As you know, we never caught the guy, and Lou has never forgiven himself for not pursuing on foot with your Mom. So yeah, you getting all the cherry gigs that other cops have been working for has a little something to do with your mom."

Nolan's knees wobbled, and he collapsed to the ground. Juice bent over to pick him up, but Nolan waved him off. He sat on the ground and choked the tears back. "Why didn't Lou pursue him on foot? It makes no sense to get back in the car."

"I don't know, Nolan. All I know is that your mom lost her life by trying to prove something and take down this guy all by herself instead of waiting for Lou. The way you showboat and want all the glory is exactly what got your mom killed." Jared picked up his grandson and embraced him with a warm hug. "Stick to the plan. Going to Rob's casino alone would've been suicide."

Nolan glanced over at Juice. Juice nodded his head and turned away. "What exactly is the plan, Grandpa?"

Jared smiled. "Find out where the drugs are coming from in the high school." He pointed at Juice. "Use him as a resource, but don't put him in any more danger than absolutely necessary." Jared turned his attention toward Juice. "Also, don't tell anyone else that Nolan is a cop or that you're an informant. You're going to get both of you killed."

"Who did you tell I was a cop?" Nolan asked.

Juice wouldn't look Nolan in the eyes. "I told my Uncle Rob that you were. He would've found out somehow. He always finds out."

Nolan sighed. "It's a good thing I didn't make it to Mesquite. I had a whole song and dance about how I hated the cops."

The three of them shared a good laugh, and all of them jumped into Jared's truck. Jared put his arm around Nolan, put it into drive, and took off.

# CHAPTER 29

Nolan wandered the halls, not making any headway on either case. He didn't want anyone talking to him, and he sure as hell didn't want to talk to anyone. He would often find himself outside by the school's greenroom. The weather was turning colder, and nobody bothered the guy who sat outside in the winter. There wasn't any snow in St. George, but it was cold enough to see your breath. He could be alone and think out there.

Most of his time spent out there was wasted. The lifters and steroid abusers didn't want anything to do with Nolan, and Lou wouldn't let him help out with Cory's murder. He was certain that Cory's killer and the drugs were connected hand in hand, but he couldn't get a firm grasp on the situation. A hooker was the last person with Cory in a sleazy motel room, and he had a giant wad of cash. If the hooker had killed him, she certainly would've taken the cash. Lou had to know that. Nothing added up in Nolan's head.

Ever since Cory's death, Ken may as well have been a ghost, and Juice's newfound love for detective work made Nolan's blood boil. Just because he's never been caught for his crimes doesn't mean he should be able to become a cop. He's still a criminal. Without Ken's help, Juice had nothing to offer besides the junkies and roiders.

Nolan sat on the steps beside the greenhouse when he felt warm hands cover his eyes.

"Guess who?"

Nolan instantly recognized the comforting soft voice. "You know I don't like to play games, Karen."

Karan sat down next to him and held his hand. "What do you like? You're kind of a party pooper. I hate to say it, but you make Oscar look like a party animal."

"Who's Oscar?" Nolan said

"Oscar the Grouch from Sesame Street. I used to love that show. My mom bought me a DVD of it when I was a little kid, and I would watch it for hours on end. When Dad watched me, that's all I would do. He didn't have a limit on how much TV I could watch, so I took full advantage of it."

Nolan had never heard Karen talk about her mom. "Did your mom have a limit on how much TV you could watch?"

Karen let go of Nolan's hand and looked away, off into the sky. "One thing I miss about Texas is that I could look in any direction and see as far as the eye could. Here in Utah there are mountains in every direction."

Nolan took her hand inside of his. Her hand looked like a doll's inside of his giant hand. "Most people prefer the mountains to plains. Instead of the same thing for miles on miles, there's new landscape around every bend."

Karen leaned her head on Nolan's shoulder. "I hate mountains. My mom likes to go rock climbing. She learned at a local rock climbing wall, and now she takes trips all over the world for her silly little hobby."

"I never really liked the mountains either. Give me a beach, surfboard, and a beer, and I'm in heaven."

Karen laughed. "A beer? I thought you were Mormon?"

"My Grandpa Jared is. He still goes to church every Sunday. I used to; but when my mom died, I stopped going."

Karen lifted her head from his shoulder. "Why?"

"I wish there was some answer that made sense to me. The most logical explanation I can come up with is that she was the one who made me go. I went for the first few weeks after her death, but then a football game was on that I wanted to watch one Sunday, so I stayed home and watched it. It was little by little, but eventually I stopped altogether. What about you? Are you a religious person?"

Karen blinked a few times. "This is where our relationship is headed? We're really going to talk about this? I'm spiritual, not religious."

"That's fair enough. I think I know exactly what you mean."

Karen stood up and put her coat on. "Walk with me to my car. I'm freezing."

Nolan got up and put his jacket on. They walked slowly toward her car, holding hands along the way. "I'm sorry about your mom dying. I would've really loved to meet the woman who molded such a great young man."

"Thanks. She was the best. I still haven't had an apple pie as good as hers. Even though Principal Bitton thinks his can give hers a run for its money. I'm sorry your mom . . . Well I'm not sure where she is, but I'm sorry you don't get to be with her."

Karen stopped in her tracks. "I've gone back and forth whether to tell you about my mom. I'm not sure on how to broach it."

"I don't need to know if you don't want to tell me. That's your family business, and that's all I need to know," Nolan said.

"Dad had an assistant coach down in Texas. The two of them were the best tandem in the state. Dad ran the defense, and Coach Mitch ran the offense. They didn't really get along that well off the football field, but on it, they were unstoppable. Football down in Texas is more than it is here. All the clichés are true. Small towns shut down on Friday nights, ten-thousand-seat stadiums are full, and the head coaches are paid more than the administrators down there. Before every season, Dad would have a local newscaster at our house talking about the upcoming season. He always invited Coach Mitch to come and be a part of it. Two years ago, before my junior year, the reporter came over and interviewed my dad and Mitch. After Dad was finished talking about the defense, the reporter turned his attention to Mitch. Instead of talking about the offense, he showed him a picture of him and my mom coming out of some hotel room. He showed him another picture of the two of them making out in the back row of the movies. Dad cold-cocked Mitch right then and there without any hesitation. Mitch fell like a sack of potatoes and was unconscious for a few seconds. Of course, the camera caught the entire thing. When the report came out, Dad and Mitch were both fired. Mom chose to shack up with that weasel, and Dad came out here. Mom wanted me to stay with her, but she can go to hell. She might as well be dead."

Nolan rubbed the back of his neck with his right hand. "Did Mitch bleed?"

Karen's head turned towards Nolan, and they both began to crack up. "No, I think he pissed himself when he got knocked out; but to his credit, he didn't bleed. He must have tough skin."

Nolan grabbed Karen's hand again, and they strolled along the parking lot. "I know you're mad at your mom right now, but you can always pick up the phone and call her anytime. Keep that in mind. It may be your lifeline one day."

# CHAPTER 30

Nolan's cell phone rang, Chris Ledoux's "Hooked on an Eight Second Ride." He made that Juice's ringtone because being in business with him was like riding a bull; you hold on as tight as you can and hope you don't get trampled. It also didn't hurt that Juice couldn't stand country music. Juice always grumbled for Nolan to change his ringtone. He looked at the phone for a second. He finally pressed the green button.

"What's going on, Juice?"

"Hey, Noles. Our main man Ken wants to have a meeting with you tonight. I told him he could do it at my parents', but he wants to do it at his place. Is that cool with you?"

"Yeah, man. Whatever you think is best," Nolan said.

"What I think is best is we bust this fool, and I go to the academy ASAP."

"You know you have to have a clean record and graduate high school before you'll get accepted?"

"I know. If it wasn't for you and your undercover work, I would be out of the slinging business without getting any felonies, and I plan on graduating early. I want to get on with my training.

"How are you going to graduate early? You're never in class. The only time I see you in school is in the parking lot or lunchroom."

"It's all good, Noles. Dixie State College offers a GED program at night. I already dropped out of Red Rock High and enrolled in the classes. I should be able to pass my GED in January."

"Well good for you, I guess. If you have dropped out of school, how come you're always there?"

"We got work to do, bro. We need to find out who killed Cory and bust Ken's pasty ass while we're at it," Juice said.

"I have work to do. You're the informant. You inform me if anything is going on. You don't do any busting. You also got it backwards. I need to find out who's supplying Ken, and if I come across who killed Cory, that's a bonus."

There was silence on the other end. Nolan waited for Juice to say something, anything, when a deep, dark voice came through the line. "Let me tell you something, Nolan. Cory may have been a woman beater, drug dealer, and steroid abuser, but there were things about him that weren't all that bad. In fact, they were good traits for anyone to have. When Karen ripped my heart out, he was there for me as a friend and not only listened but encouraged my crazy schemes to get her back. He left football, a sport he loved more than anything, when I did because I asked him to. And he picked a fight with you because I wanted to see how tough you were. Cory may have been a lot of things, but he was always loyal to me. Getting to know you these past few months, Nolan, I only know for certain one thing about you. You look at everything in black and white. Cory wasn't all black; there was some white in there. Like most people, including you, Nolan, he was grey."

"Tell Ken I'll be at his place at 8:00 p.m. Text me his address." Nolan hung up the phone. He walked downstairs and made himself a turkey sandwich. He opened the fridge and saw the Dijon mustard. His mom used to always put Dijon mustard on his sandwiches. He never liked it and didn't have the heart to tell her. Since her passing, he always found himself putting it on.

He finished eating and left a note for his grandpa on the table. "Grandpa, going to put in some work tonight. Don't worry about supper, I already ate."

Nolan got into his old Honda, rolled down the window, and put it in reverse. He checked his phone to see if Juice had texted him the address yet. He recognized the address. It was where his best friend Henny growing up lived. He didn't know if his parents still lived there, but he couldn't risk being seen by them. When he pulled up to Ken's apartment complex, he pulled a beanie on and pulled his jacket collar up over his jaw. Then he put his sunglasses on and marched up to apartment 2C. Nolan banged on the door and waited. Ken opened the door and stepped to the side to let him in. Ken's apartment wasn't anything special, one bedroom, one bathroom, brown carpet, and a living room that connected to a tiny kitchen. All in all, it's what a twenty-two-year-old who worked at a school should live in. No extravagant purchases from his dealing other than his truck.

"Why are you banging my door down? I thought Swat was coming in." Ken looked at him crooked. "Why are you dressed like that?"

"Why do you think? The last thing I want is someone recognizing me going to a drug deal."

Ken rolled his eyes. "This isn't a drug deal. It's a discussion. As of late, Juice has really been hitting me up trying to get you in on some more products. I'm not sure how I feel about it."

Nolan took his sunglasses and hat off. "I delivered for you with the steroids in two days. Why are you having second thoughts about me?"

Ken went to the kitchen and cracked a cold Budweiser. "You want one?"

Nolan sat down at the table. "Sure."

Ken reached into his fridge and tossed him the beer. Nolan opened it up and took a big swig. Then he leaned back in his chair and took another drink. Ken sat down across the table from him. "There's something about you, Nolan, that I don't understand. You're not a mystery, I'm fairly certain I've got you figured out, but something doesn't seem right about you. Like how long have you been drinking beer?"

"Since my mom died," Nolan said.

"When did she die?" Ken asked.

"Almost five years ago."

Ken put both his elbows on the table and stared into Nolan's soul. "That's what I can't figure out about you Nolan. You're eighteen years old, and you've been drinking since you were thirteen. Something doesn't add up to me. The way you chugged those beers, I have no doubt that you've been drinking for five years."

He'd had some close calls while he was at Red Rock High almost blowing his cover, but this was the first time that he hadn't seen it coming. Ken and his beers was clever. Nolan knew he couldn't underestimate Ken. Ken and Cory were polar opposites when it came to smarts. Ken used his, Cory didn't. Nolan stared right back into Ken's eyes, fire burning through his veins. They were like two lions about to determine who was going to eat the zebra for dinner.

"Quit beating around the bush, Ken. If you have something on your mind, spit it out. If not, let's talk business," Nolan said.

"Ever since you showed up in the hallways, lost like a puppy dog, things in my world seem to be more complicated. I usually don't let kids form high school get to me, but you . . . I don't believe you're only eighteen years old."

Nolan stood up and turned around. He didn't want Ken to see him squirm. He searched his mind for the next words that came out of his mouth. He knew he had to say the exact right thing for Ken to never bring this up again. Nolan stalled. "What makes you say that?"

Ken opened another beer. "A couple of things, really. Principal Bitton has met one-on-one with you way too many times, and your Grandpa Jared is a well-respected man in the community. I know this isn't a one-horse town, but it's not Los Angeles either. It was big news when the former police chief's daughter was killed in the line of duty. That was damn near five years ago. I remember reading her obituary. Her eighteen-year-old son named Nolan and her father, Jared, were left behind. That is quite the coincidence that your grandpa's name is Jared and your name is Nolan."

Nolan had only one hand to play so he played it. "You're right, that was my mom. And my grandpa was the police chief many years ago. You're even right about that eighteen-year-old kid being me. I faked my transcripts and moved in with my grandpa, who has Alzheimer's, just to go to Red Rock High.

Ken's head almost exploded. He chugged what was left of his beer.

"Why would you want to go to Red Rock High? You would need a pretty elaborate scheme to get fake transcripts past Principal Bitton."

"No, not an elaborate scheme. Just a damn good forgery, and there isn't anyone better in Utah at counterfeiting documents than me."

Ken rubbed his forehead with his thumb and index finger. "That still doesn't answer my question about wanting to come to Red Rock. There's not a single reason for you to be back in high school unless you're a nark."

Nolan had to swing for the fences with his next lie. "It's because of you, Ken. I knew who you were before you knew who I was. I knew that you were the player in this town. I also knew that you worked at the school more than full time. This was my way of becoming one of your soldiers."

Nolan turned around and held his breath. This was the moment of truth. If Ken didn't buy what Nolan was selling, then his time as an undercover at Red Rock would be over.

"I still don't understand why you're pretending to be a student? That seems like a total cop move. Now that I know who your mom and grandpa were, it's not a far leap to assume that you're a cop," Ken said.

"How else was I going to make contact with you? Apply to be Rocco's assistant coach? Should I have seen if the school needed another hall monitor, janitor, or lunch lady? This was the best way to get into it. After I had earned your trust, I was going to quit school and make money hands over fist working full time for you. As far as my family's history goes with law enforcement, why would I want to take a job that killed my mom and ruined my grandfather's life?"

"So after you became a student, why didn't you find me out and ask for a job? Why all the hanging out with Juice and hostility towards Cory?"

Nolan was so deep into the lie he didn't even need to think about it anymore, words just flowed naturally. "What was I going to say to you? Hi Ken, I know you're a really good drug dealer, and I want to join you. You would've run me out of the school that day. Juice was a means to an end. I knew the second I met him that he was on your payroll. The steroids, weed, and his attitude were all a dead giveaway. And Cory . . . he rubbed me the wrong way, so I wanted to kick his ass."

Ken stood up from the table. "It's a convincing story, but I don't know if I believe you or not. Let me make a few phone calls. What's your last name and social security number?"

"Nolan Smith, 856-44-9576. Go ahead and check me out. My story will match."

Ken snatched his phone off the table and shut the door to his bedroom. Nolan sat down on the couch and took his gun off safety and put it in his front pocket of his hoodie. Nolan grabbed his phone and checked to see if he had any messages. Karen left him a text, but nothing from Juice or anything important to the case. Twenty minutes later, Ken came out of his bedroom. Nolan slipped his hand inside his pocket and grabbed his gun. He had to be ready for anything Ken threw at him. Ken came out with a gallon Ziploc bag full of weed.

"I called my guy. You have a pretty unspectacular background. Dropped out of UNLV after one year, been to the drunk tank a few times, even served thirty days for domestic violence against an old girlfriend. Does Karen know about that?"

Nolan took his hand out of his hoodie. "How the hell do you know about that?"

"What did you think I was doing in my bedroom? I got more guys than you can imagine. It took me ten minutes to run your background." Ken tossed the bag of weed to Nolan. "Sell this by the end of the week. Thirty dollars for a dime, twenty dollars for a nickel. If you show me you can do that, then you can be one of my soldiers."

"Consider it done," Nolan said.

"One more thing, Nolan. I don't want to see you at the school anymore. You got your job, now go sell. Don't waste my or your time on classes anymore. I know you have your thing with Karen. On a side note, you're lucky she's nineteen years old . . . otherwise that shit would be creepy. But you need to come up with a reason you're not going to be at school anymore."

Nolan nodded his head, put his sunglasses back on, and pulled his beanie over his head. He walked out the door, got into his car, and pulled away. He made sure that no one followed him. He pulled over and called Lou. When there was no answer, he left a message.

"Lou, I'm in with Ken. By the way, nice backstory on me. You put some serious thought into it. You changing my background is the only reason Ken believed me. It's not all good news though. We have a rat in our department."

# CHAPTER 31

The following morning, Lou came over to Jared's house. Nolan entered in his pajama pants, a white T-shirt, and his hair sticking up everywhere.

"Why would you say that we have a rat on the job?" Lou grabbed a cup of coffee and paced back and forth through Jared's kitchen

"Because we have a two-faced liar in the department, and you need to figure it out," Nolan said.

"So I'm just supposed to take your word for it? You say we have a rat, and I need to investigate. You need to realize who you're giving orders to. I'm your boss, not the other way around."

"I was with Ken last night. I gave him my social security number and name. He came back with the background I assume you made for my undercover identity."

"Anyone with a computer could've googled your name and social. That doesn't mean we have someone working for Ken."

Nolan caught a glimpse of Jared hiding around the corner. "What do you think, Grandpa? I gave Ken my social security number, could anybody with a computer have found that detailed of fake information?"

Jared sat on the living room couch. He sighed deeply and crossed his left leg over his right. "Could anyone have done it? I don't think so. It would've taken someone with something more than just basic computer skills. They would've had to know how to run a background check. However, that doesn't mean there's a snitch in the building. If I were you two, and I thank the good Lord everyday I'm not, I would only have communication with each other about the case. That way if there is someone giving out valuable information, he or she won't have access to it. Also, Lou, it wouldn't hurt to keep an extra eye out."

Lou went over and kissed Jared's bald spot on top of his head. "That's why this man is the best. We'll start our new protocol right now. No information to anyone but me."

Lou burst out the door faster than the roadrunner, and in the blink of an eye he was gone. Nolan, still sitting at the kitchen table, cracked open a can of soda. Jared read the morning paper. Nolan stood up and wandered over to the living room. Jared's eyes peered over his newspaper for half a second and then continued on reading. Nolan tapped his finger on the chair softly and continued to progressively get louder and louder. Jared went into the kitchen and poured himself a cup of coffee.

"Do your church buddies know that you drink that?"

"It's decaf. Don't ever mock me again, or I'll slap that pretty little smile right off your face."

"Whoa, Grandpa. I was just fooling around. You know how I don't like silence."

Jared set his coffee on the counter. "I know, Nolan. I knew that you'd have a hard time living here again, but I didn't realize how hard of a time I was going to have with it. You're running off to drug deals late at night, you're dating a high school girl, and your informant wants to join the academy."

"It's all part of the job, Gramps. You should know that better than anyone."

"I do. Believe me, I do. But I went through the same thing when your mother told me she wanted to be a cop. It's hard to sit on the sideline and hope that you do the right thing. Let's call a spade a spade. You don't go by the book very often."

"Going by the book doesn't net the results I need," Nolan said.

"Bullshit," Jared said.

Nolan sat up a little straighter. His Grandpa Jared didn't cuss too often in anger; but when he did, everyone knew it was time to listen. Jared continued, "The reason they call it the book is because these are tried and effective results. I understand not every case is the same, and you have to do some outside-the-box thinking, but you fight logic and rules around every bend. If you started your career by the book, it wouldn't have taken you almost dying in a warehouse at the hands of a crazy mobster to get you to follow some basic rules."

Nolan closed his eyes and dropped his face in the palms of his hands. "That day still haunts me. I thought

I was going to die that night, and all for what? To catch a few criminals." Nolan began weeping.

Jared went and sat beside him. He put his arm around him and let Nolan cry into his chest. After a few minutes, Nolan calmed down. "Listen, son. I'm here for you. You were given a second chance. It's more than a miracle that the mobster's lynch man was an undercover agent. You had an angel on your shoulder that night, and she protected you from anything serious."

Nolan looked at the picture of his mother that his grandpa kept above the fireplace. "Yeah, she was there that night."

"Nolan, it's really important that you run any and all information through me. Lou doesn't want to believe it, but there is somebody leaking information."

Nolan wiped his eyes. "How do you know that?"

"The fake background on you was all my handiwork. I snuck into Lou's office and downloaded that backstory. I was police chief there for thirteen years, and I knew that someone would look into your background sooner rather than later."

"Snuck into Lou's office? I thought you were a by-the-book kind of guy."

Jared ruffled his grandson's hair. "I'm a protect-my-family kind of guy first. So Ken looked at your background. What does he want you to do?"

"Well, he knows my real age. He's smart. He put your name and mom's name together and figured out who I was. He wants me to drop out of school and focus on selling immediately."

Jared jumped up and down in the same place. It was how he processed information and how he figured out what the next move would be. "I agree with Ken. You sucked at school anyways. You're not going to waste another second of your time in that school. We got the dealer, your informant is one of his soldiers, now it's time to earn some trust. You need to sell his steroid, weed, and meth . . . whatever he gives to you. You need to sell the product as fast as you can. Once you become a solid earner for him, he'll introduce you to the supplier."

Nolan put a pillow behind his head and plopped down on it. "Sell it? Like to actual junkies?"

"Yeah. This is where Juice comes into play. He needs to stop working for Ken right now. Juice told me he dropped out of high school to get his GED early, so he won't have to see Ken at school. I'll change his cell phone number, and he needs to move in with us for a couple of months. I know his stepfather really well. I'm going to flat out tell him what's going on with Juice."

"Why does he have to move in with us though?"

"I need Juice to become a ghost. If he's living with us, Ken can't track him down. It will only be for a couple of months, and you can take over his old clients. This way you won't have to track down new leads for the drugs. He'll gift wrap them to you."

Nolan nodded his head. "You're pretty good at this police stuff, aren't you?"

"Not as good as I should be after forty years on the job. Remember, Nolan, it's important to run everything by me first. From here on out, I'm your partner, not your grandpa, and I'm pulling seniority on you."

"We're going to get these guys, aren't we?" Nolan said with a giant grin on his face.

"We're going to nail their butts to the wall. Make the phone call to Juice. I'm going to go over and talk to the good judge right now."

Jared got on his bike and started to pedal away. Nolan ran out the front door and screamed, "You're riding your bike over? That has to be at least a fifteen-mile ride."

Jared smiled. "It's closer to twenty. It will give me plenty of time to figure out how to explain to a judge that his stepson was a drug dealer and now wants to be a cop. I also have to slip into the conversation that I want him to live with me for the next few months. So I think a bike ride is just what I need right now."

Nolan waved at his grandpa and went back inside. He turned the TV on and tried to watch a football game. Alabama versus Auburn in the Iron Bowl would've usually gotten his adrenaline pumping, but today he was too excited to pretend to care about the game. With the help of Jared and Juice, he felt like the case was finally going to crack for him. He scrolled through his phone while the game was on in the background. He heard the door shut and looked up.

Ken stood inside his doorframe. "Who's winning?"

# CHAPTER 32

*P*atting his own body down, Nolan felt his gun tucked away in the waistband of his jeans. He stood up and walked over to the doorway.

"Come on in."

"Was that your Grandpa riding his bike?"

"Yeah."

"Does he know it's December?"

"He's a tough old bird. He grew up in Nephi, so there is no winter for him in St. George. It's either too hot or too damn hot for him."

Ken bumped past Nolan and up the stairs. When Ken got out of sight, Nolan checked his gun was loaded. He clicked in a bullet to the chamber, put the gun back in his pants, and went up the stairs.

Ken loomed at the top of the stairs looking at family pictures. "Is this your mom?" Ken asked.

"Yeah, that's her."

"Blonde hair and blue eyes gets me every time. I would let her use her handcuffs on me for sure."

Nolan felt like his blood was literally boiling inside his body. He walked calmly up the stairs. "If you ever talk about my mom again, I'm going to skin you alive and let coyotes pick at your bones."

Ken laughed. "That's a little graphic for my liking, but it's good to see that you have some fire inside you. Most the time when I insult a loved one of my employees, they either take it or go completely nuts. It takes a special state of mind to keep your cool while also getting your point across. Well done, Nolan."

Ken opened the door to Nolan's room. He glanced around. "This is about what I expected," Ken said.

Nolan scrunched his brow. "Oh yeah, why's that?"

"You're a screw up. So naturally you have a picture of yourself playing football in college. It is impressive that you played at UNLV though. Not many kids get D1 scholarships from Utah. Tell me something though. You obviously played as a freshman, how did you screw up so bad that they wouldn't even let you come back for your sophomore year?"

Nolan didn't know what to say. The truth was, Nolan left his playing because he wanted to pursue a career as a cop, but he didn't know how much insight Ken had. He had an insider at the St. George PD; he could very easily have one inside the athletics department at UNLV.

"I didn't screw up. I left the team by choice."

Ken ruffled through some of the contents of Nolan's dresser desk. He flipped through a couple of pages of a *Sports Illustrated* and finally looked up.

"Don't hold out on me, Nolan. I know for a fact you were kicked out of UNLV. One of the perks I have of being me.

*Oh no, the background check*, Nolan thought. He forgot about the fake identity that his grandpa created for him.

"I left the team because it interfered with hunting. I got kicked out of school because I went hunting and my GPA dropped below UNLV standards."

"Huh, that's too bad. I hoped there would have been some elaborate cheating scandal, or you knocked up the coach's daughter . . . something with some excitement to it."

Nolan sat down at his computer. "Life isn't a TV show, Ken. Thousands of kids get kicked out of universities every semester because of grades."

"That's true. A couple of kids I started the teaching program with at Dixie State dropped out already."

Nolan shook his head. "I see you're still telling that lie."

"What lie would that be?" Ken asked.

"That you're becoming a teacher."

"It's not a lie. I don't want to be a drug supplier when I'm in my fifties. This is enough to get me some financial freedom. I don't want to be like Coach Porter living in some shitty two-bedroom, one-bathroom for the rest of my life. Hell, he's one of the higher-paid teachers at Red Rock High because of his coaching bonus, and he still lives in that hellhole. Besides, I already have kids on the team who buy testosterone from me. Why would I let that whale dry up?"

"I thought you were smarter than to sling drugs to students. A teacher distributing to kids is beyond stupid. When I approached you, I thought you ran a smoother ship than that."

"I don't sell them anything other than the roids. I'm sure you had a coach approach you at some point offering them."

Nolan remembered one of his position coaches in college encouraging him to start using steroids and that he had a connection. "I guess you're right. It's part of the football culture, I guess. You still should be super careful. One of those kids is going to tell someone the wrong thing, and before you know it, you'll be making reservations for the state pen."

Ken rubbed his hands together. "I'm glad you said that. This is where you come in. I'm giving you the testosterone market. You've done some good things with that in the past, so now is your chance to make some real coin. You'll work with Juice, but I'm tired of that kid using my product for his own gains. If he wants to continue to use my steroids, he's going to have to pay like everyone else."

"Oh shit," Nolan blurted out.

Ken looked at him crooked. "Oh shit, what?"

*Did I say that out loud*, Nolan thought. "It's Juice. He and his stepdad had a fight, and I told him he could crash with me for a couple of weeks."

"I'm not sure what the problem is. In fact, this works out for the best. He can sell weed to the hippies and stoners still, and you'll get his names and contacts for the muscleheads. It's actually a win-win for me."

"I don't want him to be mad at me for stealing his territory," Nolan said.

"Steal his territory? This isn't the Jets and the Sharks. I get my orders from the higher-ups, and I distribute them out as I see fit. We're a business, and we're a profitable one at that."

Nolan had a puzzled look on his face.

"What is it?" Ken asked.

"Who are the Jets and the Sharks?"

"West Side Story, only one of the greatest movies ever. Geez son, you need to get some culture into your life. Once you do, you can take down all this sports crap from you room and join the rest of us out of high school."

"Until yesterday, I was in high school. I was trying to convince people I was actually in high school."

"It's more than that," Ken said. "With the exception of you in a UNLV uniform, everything in this room screams, 'I peaked in high school, and I'm not going to change it.'"

"I guess it could use some updating," Nolan said.

Ken left the room and went downstairs. Nolan followed him to the door and opened it up. Ken bent over and pulled a bag out of the milk box sitting on the front porch. He tossed it to Nolan. Nolan saw syringes filled up.

"That's two hundred dollars' worth of testosterone. I want you to get three hundred for it. If you do that, then we can talk about some serious money."

"I can deliver, no problem," Nolan said.

Ken stepped off the porch toward his car. He turned back and looked at Nolan. "What did Juice and the judge get into a fight about?"

"Wouldn't say, but I suspect the judge knows what Juice has been doing to make a little extra money on the side."

Ken nodded his head. "Nice. I never liked the judge. He needed to be knocked off his pedestal. I would've loved to see the look on his face when he realized he had a drug dealer living in his house."

"Yeah, it would've been pretty epic." Nolan turned back into his house. "Jackass," he murmured.

# CHAPTER 33

The phone rang off the hook. Jared finally pulled his bike over to the sidewalk and looked at the caller ID. *What could Nolan want?* Jared unclicked his straps and took off his bike helmet. He put the phone up to his ear.

"What's good, my boy?"

Nolan huffed and grasped for air on the other end of the phone. "Grandpa, Ken came by. He knows."

"Settle down, Nolan. Take some deep breaths, control your breathing, and talk to me like a man. What does Ken know?"

He heard an ear-piercing scream on the other side of the phone so loud that Jared had to take the phone off his ear. After a few minutes of waiting until Nolan's temper tantrum was over, Nolan began speaking in a soft, faint voice.

"He knows a lot, Grandpa. He knows who you are and what you used to do, he knows about mom and her death, he knows where we live, and he knows Juice is living with us. He knows damn near everything."

Jared sighed. He put his phone down on the grass next to the sidewalk. He punched the tree that he parked his bike by.

"Shit."

He shook his hand off. He never could control his compulsive anger. He picked the phone up with his left hand and continued shaking out his right one.

"Nolan, you still there?"

"Yeah Grandpa, I'm still here."

"Why was he at our house?" Jared asked.

"He came to bring me some steroids to sell. He seemed to be ecstatic about Juice living with us. When I told him, he smirked, and it sent chills down my spine."

"I wouldn't read too much into that Nolan. I think he's glad he tracked Juice down. From my talk I had with Juice and his family, he's been trying to steer clear of Ken. They're only communicating over the phone."

"Juice's parents are on board with Juice moving in with us?"

"It took some convincing, but his mom thought if he really wanted to be a police officer, moving in with us would be the best. It would keep him from dealing drugs, at least."

"I don't know about that. Ken has big plans for Juice to sell the street drugs and me the steroids."

"That kid has a game plan, I'll give him that. I broke the cardinal rule that I told you to never break. I underestimated this punk. But from everything you've told me he, he doesn't know you're a cop."

"How can you be so sure of that? He's brilliant. He's figured everything out so far," Nolan said.

"That's how I can be so sure. If he's as smart as we think he is, he would never bring you actual drugs."

"What if he was setting me up?" Nolan asked.

"If he was, he wouldn't have shown up at our house. He would've called you to meet up, and then he would drop the hammer."

"This is way more intense than I thought when I signed up to be a nark in a high school. I don't think I can do this anymore."

"Stop the bawl-baby-pity-party. I need you to realize that this isn't a Russian gangster who's going to torture you. Ken is a small-time, small-town, and small-dealer loser. I need the old Nolan to come back, and in a hurry. I want the cocky guy who walked into an abandoned warehouse without any backup and wanted to kick butt. Not the false bravado know-it-all that's been in high school the past four months."

This was the first time in his entire life that Jared laid the tough love on Nolan. Jared didn't know if Nolan was going to return to the man who was too dumb to realize he was in danger or the boy who was beating up high school kids to prove he was still the man. He hung on the line, not knowing what response Nolan was going to give.

He paced up and down the sidewalk when he spotted kids playing on the slides at the park across the street. They didn't have a care in the world. He remembered when he took Nolan to that park with his mom every Sunday. Even when his mom was on duty, she would meet them there. The view of the mountains wasn't redder in any other part of the state. There were blue spruce pine trees covering the red mountains. There wasn't anywhere in the world that had the blue-on-red look. The blue spruces made Jared smile and reminisce of his childhood up north. He could look up toward the Wasatch mountain range for hours right outside his childhood bedroom window. Maybe that's why he always insisted on going to that park. Even then Nolan had the attitude of the toughest kid on the playground. He was the kid other parents warned their kids about, not to steal his toys. Eventually Jared stopped going to the park to spare himself from the embarrassment of another parent scolding him about Nolan's behavior. Jared got back on the phone.

"Alright Gramps, I can be that guy again. We're going to need to protect Juice since Ken knows where he's at now."

"Juice doesn't need any protection from us. I would go into the lion's den with that kid any day. I can almost guarantee that Ken is the one scared of Juice. If anything, I'm looking forward to Juice protecting me."

Jared hung up the phone and pedaled back toward his house. He stopped and paused at the park. For an instant, he was sure he could see Nolan on the swings getting pushed by his mom.

*It's time to finish what we started*, Nolan thought. *How could Jared have more faith in Juice than he had in his own grandson?* Nolan sulked on his bed, tossing a baseball up in the air to himself. Lost in his own thoughts, Nolan re-ran the last four months in his head. *I found Juice and made him my informant, I beat Cory to a pulp, I made Ken trust me. I'm the one who Grandpa should be drooling all over.*

Nolan riffled the baseball at his wall. He put a giant hole in the drywall. *Great, I'm sure Grandpa would rather have Juice fix the wall now,* Nolan thought. He yanked his jacket off the hanger and ran downstairs. He got into his car and took off.

He pulled up to Karen's house and sat in her driveway with the car turned off. He cranked up his stereo and laid back his seat. Meditation was the only thing that put Nolan in the right frame of mind. Some people think it needs to be quiet to meditate, but Nolan found out quickly that he was way more dangerous when he was alone with his own mind. Metallica, AC/DC, and Guns N' Roses were more than enough to clear his mind. Something about rock music soothed Nolan's soul. The guitars, the drumming, the lyrics all made sense to him.

He closed his eyes and listened and pondered. He knew he needed to get back to the guy that his grandpa needed, but he couldn't turn off his fear like he could a light switch. On one hand, his grandpa told him he needs to use his head and be safe. He'd been chewed out by Lou and his grandpa about being reckless more times than he could even count. Now his grandpa wanted the ass-kicker back?

Tapping on Nolan's window awakened him. Coach Porter stared at him like a pit bull would stare at a fresh piece of meat. He motioned for Nolan to roll down the window. Nolan sat up and rolled it down.

"Music is a little loud, wouldn't you say?" Porter asked.

"Sorry, sir. Music is how I deal with things. It helps me relax."

"Why couldn't you deal with your shit in your own driveway? It's not exactly the middle of the night, but it's also not mid-afternoon. People are sitting down to dinner, and they have to hear 'Enter Sandman'?"

"You know Metallica?"

"I've been a coach for twenty years. I've heard as much Metallica as James Hetfield."

Nolan scratched the back of his head. "Who's that?"

"Really? You claim to be a fan of his and don't even know him? He's the lead singer of Metallica." Coach Porter's face got red really quick, and he opened the car door. He about tore it off the frame. "What the hell are we even talking about? What are you doing in my driveway?"

"Karen has been my rock since I've started dating her. She is always the one with a level head. I need her advice?"

Coach Porter unbuckled Nolan and jerked him out of the car by his shirt.

"Then turn off the damn music, fix your hair, and go talk to her."

Nolan shoved Coach Porter's hands off of him. "Don't put your hands on me, tough guy," Nolan smirked.

Coach Porter shook his head. "I'm not sure what you're so happy about, but if you ever talk to me like that again, I'm putting you on your ass. Understood?"

Nolan nodded his head. "Do you care if I go in and see Karen?"

Dumbfounded, Coach Porter didn't know what to say. Nolan was a snot-nosed punk, but he did have some newfound guts, and Porter could always appreciate that.

"In the living room, and keep your hands off her."

Nolan sprinted into their house and called out for Karen to come down. Karen came down from her room. Nolan still couldn't believe she was dating him. Every time she turned the corner, she stunned him more and more. He was more than infatuated with her, he loved her.

"I came here for you to fix my dilemma, but I'm pretty sure that your dad took care of it," Nolan said.

"Daddy isn't the type of guy who is going to put his arm around you and listen to your problems."

"He has no idea that he fixed me. But his abrasive nature is just the type of thing that I needed."

"Why don't you run your troubles by me anyways?"

Nolan gulped. "My grandpa needs me to be the old me, but not exactly the old me. A version of me that is safe but reckless, hands out pain but gets no pleasure from it. I need to be yin and yang."

Karen put her palm in her face. "You need to talk like a human and not some kind of robot. I'm not sure what you just said."

"I went through some hell about six months ago. I'm not going to go into what happened, but let's just say I was going to meet my mom sooner than I expected."

"You almost died? Is that what you're saying to me?"

"Yeah."

"What was it? A car crash, nearly drowned, hunting accident?"

"It doesn't matter. I put myself into a position that I shouldn't have. Ever since then I have been floating around petrified of all things compromising."

"That's not exactly true. You literally beat up Cory, and you became Juice's number one. That's not exactly someone who's petrified. In fact, I'm not sure you even know what that means."

Nolan had a blank stare on his face. "Those things don't make you brave, or some kind of tough guy. Cory, God rest his soul, was a typical high school bully. I knew I could kick his ass anytime I wanted to. And if I couldn't, I knew he couldn't kill me if push came to shove. The worst he could do to me is a few bumps and bruises."

Karen's brain was spinning a million miles an hour as she processed the information as quickly as she could, but she got caught up on the words Nolan said. "Kill you. Of course no high school fight in the lunchroom ends up in death. What type of trouble were you in six months ago?"

"It was bad. The only thing you need to know is that I came over here bummed out that my own grandpa thought Juice could do more for him than I could. Now I know I can step up to the plate."

"And my dad said something to you to help you realize that?"

"No, your dad is a dick. He pulled me out of my car like a grizzly pulls salmon out of an Alaskan river. But instead of backing down like I thought I would, I pushed him off of me. It was the classic fight or flight, and I fought. I know when my grandpa needs me, I will always fight for him."

Karen plopped onto the couch. "That's good I guess. I was going to rent a movie. Do you want to stay and watch it? We'll order some dinner and make a whole thing out of it."

Nolan slid in right next to her. "As long as it's not a chick flick. It seems like the only movies I've ever watched with you are chick flicks."

Karen laughed. "Okay, you can pick the show, but nothing too bloody or scary. How about a comedy that has a love story in it?"

"You want a romantic comedy? Or in other words, a chick flick?"

Karen smiled and, as always, it rocked Nolan's world. He scrolled through the choices and found one that fit Karen's criteria.

"Are you happy?" Nolan asked.

"Extremely happy." Karen put her head down on Nolan's lap and put her feet on the rest of the couch.

"Nolan, can I ask you one more question?"

"Sure."

"What did my dad do when you pushed his hands off of you?"

"He told me he would beat me within an inch of my life if I ever put my hands on him again."

Karen slipped her shoes off. "It's a good thing he gave you a warning. He must like you?"

"He doesn't like me. He made it very clear by threatening me."

"If he didn't like you, he wouldn't have said a word. He would've just left you flattened on the ground, and I would've had to clean you up. Just ask Juice."

Before the movie started, Karen was fast asleep on Nolan's lap. This was everything that Nolan wanted out of life: a good woman by his side, a job that he loved, and his confidence back. He leaned back on a pillow and closed his eyes.

# CHAPTER 34

*R* ubbing his eyes, trying to get them in focus, Nolan looked at his phone. It was 6:30 a.m. He had spent the night with Karen, and they didn't even so much as kiss. He slid out from under her head and placed it on a pillow. He tapped her on the shoulder and whispered, "I'm going home; I'll call you later."

She mumbled something and waved goodbye without her head ever leaving the pillow. Nolan tiptoed quietly toward the door, which he opened slowly.

"Why are you sneaking out of here, son?" Coach Porter said. "You're either trying to leave without saying goodbye to my daughter or you don't want to see me."

"I said bye to Karen."

"You didn't want to see me then, or you thought I didn't know you spent the night?"

Nolan's legs felt like they were a hundred pounds each. He hadn't thought about why he was sneaking out. He'd done it so many times before that it was more of a habit than anything else.

"I guess I didn't want you to know I'd spent the night."

"You come into my house, fall asleep on my couch with my daughter, and I don't hear you leave all night. You must think I'm some country dipshit, don't ya?"

"Not at all."

"Then why on God's green earth did you assume you could slip out of my house without me knowing about it. I know everything that goes on in this house. And trust me, if you would've been anywhere else besides sleeping on the couch, I would've tossed your skinny little ass out. Now I'm tired. I didn't sleep last night, so go home."

Nolan gave him a casual wave goodbye and jumped into the driver's seat. He saw Coach Porter watching him out the door. Nolan stuck two fingers out the car window and gave him the peace sign. He knew that would get under Coach Porter's skin. He and the coach were never going to see eye to eye, but he knew deep in his heart that Coach Porter realized what he needed the night before and kicked him in the pants to do it. Nolan had played for enough coaches in his lifetime to know that the best coaches know when to fire a player up or pat him on the back. From the looks of it, Coach Porter was one of the best coaches around.

Nolan parked on the curb by Jared's house. A big, yellow Ford F-150 was parked in Nolan's spot in the driveway. Juice and a couple of the kids from his weightlifting team were unloading boxes. For someone who was only staying with them for a few months, he sure had a lot of junk to unload.

Nolan got out of the car and grabbed a box. "Where are these going to?"

"Noles, it's about damn time that you showed up. Jerry and Jack have been bustin' their humps to get me moved in. Where have you been?"

"It doesn't matter. What are you doing here so early? It's Saturday. You could've moved in at any time."

Juice was in the bed of the truck sliding boxes toward the tailgate. "Not going to tell me where you were all night? I can only assume you were with Karen then."

Nolan shook his head. "I was, but it's not what you think it was. Coach stayed up all night to make sure nothing funny happened."

"You don't need to tell me, man. I spent the better half of two years over at her house. Rocco has a way about him that even I can't help but respect."

"You don't respect him. You got half the football team to quit and follow you. You hate him more than you respect him."

Juice jumped out of the bed of the truck. "Hate and respect can go hand in hand. I know that sounds bizarre, but that's how it is. Think about some of the fights you've been in. After Cory drilled you with his fastball, didn't you respect his arm strength after that? You clearly hated him, but you knew if you ever grappled again, you were going to make sure you got out of the way of anything he threw, weren't you?"

Nolan nodded his head in agreement.

"That's how it was, Rocco Porter and me. I can't stand that guy. He basically ran me off the team for dating his daughter. He told me that if I broke up with Karen I could get back on the team, even after I knocked out one of his assistant coaches. I told him I wasn't going to do that, not because I was madly in love with her, but I didn't want someone else dictating my life. He actually told me he could respect that, but his terms were his terms, so he kicked me off the team. I waited a few weeks to see if he would let me back on, but he kept to his word. I think he's an ass for doing it, but he never lied to me."

Nolan grabbed the last box and took it to the basement. Juice tossed the keys of the truck to one of his helpers and told them to drop it off at his mom's house. Juice opened the screen door and followed Nolan to the basement. They set up his room really quick. It already had a bed and desk in it, so all they needed to do was set up Juice's computer and PlayStation.

"I got a call from Ken last night after he was here," Juice said.

"Oh yeah, what did he have to say?"

"Probably the same thing he told you. You were going to take over the roids, and I was going to focus on the recreational stuff."

"We can help each other out, you know," Nolan said.

"How so?"

"You'll give me your contacts on who you sold the steroids to. That way we can keep up an appearance and make Ken some money. But we're not going to get cocaine, pot, and heroine on the streets. We have some cash stashed away at the department. We'll flush the drugs and keep Ken happy with the money. He keeps supplying us, we keep paying him, and eventually we meet the boss."

"Sounds like a solid plan to me. I don't want to be part of that life anymore."

"Hang on for a couple more weeks. We're busting Ken, no matter what. We got enough dirt on him to send him away for three to five."

"Why don't we take him right now then?" Juice asked.

"If we take him right now, there will be someone else ready to slide right in. Look at Cory. He's dead, and Ken put you into his spot and me into yours. We need to find the guy who's supplying Ken. Then we'll really have something."

"Speaking of Cory, where are we at on solving his murder?"

"Not very close, as far as I can tell. Lou's been working on it himself . . . running down leads, interviewing anyone and everyone . . . there's just not a lot to go on. It could've been anyone. A stoner looking for his fix, a domestic dispute, or Cory could've been in the wrong room at the wrong time."

"What about Ken? I wouldn't put it past him."

Nolan shook his head. "He was the first person I thought of after Cory's murder, but he has an airtight alibi. He was coaching Red Rock's game that night. He was with Coach Porter and the rest of the staff all day and night."

Juice opened up one of the boxes that they brought in. It had pounds of pot in Ziploc bags. Nolan's eyes were the size of saucers. Juice grabbed one of the bags and went toward the bathroom.

"If we're going to flush this shit, we better get going. We got some work to do."

Nolan picked up the box and took it to the bathroom. He grabbed one of the bags and dumped it in the toilet.

"How much money are we flushing away?" Nolan asked.

"Close to thirty thousand dollars' worth."

"No wonder Ken wants to sell this crap. He wouldn't have made this much his first year of teaching."

Once they finished flushing the drugs, Juice and Nolan went over what the next two weeks were going to be. Nolan needed Juice to hook him up in the world of bodybuilders, meatheads, and jocks. They needed the money from the roid ragers to keep Ken and his boss off their butts for some time.

Juice called a few of his favorite customers and set up the meet. Juice apologized to them that he couldn't get them their fix anymore, but steroid junkies didn't seem to care where it came from. As long as they had the same magic medicine, they were satisfied.

Nolan met the first guy outside the local college gym. He recognized him. He couldn't remember his name, but he was the baseball player who had recently been drafted. He was a local celebrity. St. George didn't have too many kids that could hit a baseball four hundred feet. They went inside to the batting cages. The kid slipped Nolan one hundred dollars. Nolan counted out the five twenty-dollar bills and put them in his pocket. Nolan opened up his gym bag and ruffled through it. He pulled out a crumpled, brown paper bag. Nolan handed him the bag, and he looked in it.

"A hundred dollars only gets ten syringes these days, huh?"

"Ten dollars a syringe is what I was told to sell them for."

They shook hands, and the kid went back to batting practice.

Juice texted the address and name of the next guy to Nolan. Nolan pulled up to an apartment complex. He wandered around for a few minutes until he found apartment 4E. He knocked on the door. A scrawny, blonde-haired man wearing a wifebeater tank top and green gym shorts two sizes too big opened the door. Nolan stepped in. "Are you Chuck?"

The skinny man answered, "Yeah. Are you Juice's guy?"

"Sure am. What can I do for you, Chuck?"

"I'm looking to bulk up."

*If there's anyone who could use this, then it's this guy*, Nolan thought.

"I can help you with that. Let me ask you a question first. Why don't you try protein shakes, weightlifting, and eating a lot of carbs first?"

"I have tried all that bullshit. I need the good stuff that Juice has. I'm tired of working out without any results."

"Fair enough. It's ten dollars a syringe. I recommend you only do five in one cycle and then take a couple of weeks off. After that you can increase the amount you can cycle."

"Give me twenty."

Juice told Nolan never to argue with the customer. Give them what they want. It wasn't his job to make sure they knew what they were doing. His only job was to get the money and get rid of the product. Nolan reluctantly counted out twenty and put them into a shoebox. The scrawny man handed Nolan twenty ten-dollar bills. Nolan grabbed his bag and speed-walked to the door. The first deal he made with the baseball star didn't leave him feeling dirty inside; but meeting at a rundown apartment complex with a loser who, only God knows why he wanted to get bigger, left him wanting a shower.

Nolan looked down to see where his next appointment was. It was the address to Red Rock High. It was Saturday, so he wasn't sure where he was supposed to go, but he pulled up into the back parking lot. He scanned around but couldn't see anyone. He put his car in drive and drove around to all the parking lots. That's when he saw Rex walking toward him.

Rex approached the car. "You're Juice's new guy? Can't say I'm surprised. It was only a matter of time before he got his clutches into you."

"Rex, where you been? I haven't seen you since you took Christy to Homecoming. You drop out of school or something?"

"Yeah, I guess you could say that. After Cory's death, I decided life was too damn short to waste my time in a classroom."

"What are you going to do with your life then? You're only sixteen years old. No degree, no skill, and someone who makes poor choices isn't exactly what the workforce is looking for."

"The workforce can kiss my butt. I'm training to be a professional bodybuilder. Some of those guys make upwards of ten grand a show. After that the World's Strongest Man competition is calling my name. "

Nolan chuckled. "Sounds like a solid plan. I don't see any flaws in it."

Rex slipped him a hundred-dollar bill. "Just fill my order. I'm not looking for any advice from Juice's bitch."

Nolan clenched his fist and cracked his knuckles. He jumped out of the car and got in Rex's face. Jared's words rang through his head as soon as he got out of the car. "There's a difference between being tough and pretending to be tough by knocking out high schoolers." Nolan backed away and stuck his head in his car window. He grabbed his bag on the front seat of his car and counted out ten. He gave them to Rex and got back into his car.

"Hey Rex, I know you're not looking for advice, but let me give you some anyways. You can compete in amateur competitions while going to school. Because even if you become the world's strongest man or the best bodybuilder, you can only do that until your body breaks down. After that, you'll need to find a real job."

"Not if I make millions doing it, dumb-ass."

Nolan rolled his eyes. "You're right. If you make millions of dollars, then you won't need an education."

Nolan burnt the tires out and was off. He took the long way home. This was the first time he had to really think about what he did. For the first time in his life, he did true undercover work. He knew some of the players in the drug world, and he knew Ken was a dangerous man who needed to be removed from Red Rock High.

Nolan pulled up to his house where Jared and Juice were sitting on the porch swing. They were laughing and slapping each other's back. Nolan leaned on the pillar next to the porch.

"What are you two giggling like little school girls about?"

"Ah Noles, you know, this and that. Your Grandpa Jared, a.k.a. J-man, is a pretty cool dude. He's been telling me about some of his glory days. There's a shitload." Juice looked at Jared, embarrassed. "I mean, a boatload of murders in our city over the years."

"Whoa, when did you stop cussing?" Nolan asked.

"J-man told me that swearing shows my education level. If I can't come up with a better word, then I need to crack the dictionary to come up with one."

"What did he tell you about giving everyone you meet a goofy nickname?"

Juice looked at Jared and Nolan and put his head down. Jared chimed in, "I like J-man. It makes me feel like I'm fifty-five again. It gets my blood pumping."

Nolan looked over at Juice and saw a smile creep over his face.

"So how did today go?" Jared asked.

Nolan pulled out the cash and put it on the swing. "I can see why people do this. I made four hundred dollars in less than an hour."

"Correction, Noles. You made about fifty dollars. You're going to give that money to Ken, and he'll throw you a bone, usually around ten percent. Then he's going to give it to his boss, who will give him around twenty-five percent, so about one hundred dollars. Then that greedy prick will take the rest."

"So I get the least amount of money for doing all the work? Something doesn't seem right about that."

Jared stood up and stretched his legs out. "Welcome to the crazy and exciting world of drugs. Come to think of it, it's really not that different from the business world. The

CEO's delegate to the managers, the manager's delegate to the laborers, and the cycle goes round and round."

Nolan turned his attention toward Juice. "Should we call Ken and give him the money?"

"Not for four hundred dollars. We need to sell about sixty more syringes before we call. Once you have a thousand dollars, that will get his attention. When we have his attention, then we can make our move."

"What if I take the rest of the money from the evidence locker? That way we can meet with him tonight."

"What the hell am I going to give him then? I need that money for the drugs I flushed down the toilet. We need to be patient."

"I agree with Juice," Jared said. "There's a difference between being a good salesman and being suspiciously quick."

"Listen to your grandpa on this one, Noles. Besides, Ken knows all of the steroid clients. He knows when they'll need a new cycle. That's going to take at least one more week to get the players we need."

Nolan sat down on the stairs leading up to the porch. "We need to get this guy off the street and soon."

"Why the hurry all of a sudden, son?" Jared asked.

"Being out there and seeing who actually purchases these drugs gave me a rude awakening. The kid who was just drafted for baseball was the first client of the day."

Juice nodded in agreement. "Drew, oh yeah. That kid is a baller. Baseball ain't my thing in particular, but I could watch that kid drill the ball all day."

"Yeah, and we're ruining his chance at the show for a few bucks."

"What you mean ruining? Before I found that kid, he was a weak-hitting shortstop. He could always put the ball in play, but I gave him the power. I say I made his life." Jared sat back down next to Juice and put his arm around him. "You may have given him that little extra he needed, but you did it illegally. Now since it's baseball and everyone and their dog does steroids, he may benefit from them. But you need to change your way of thinking if the academy is in your future."

Nolan, still on his soapbox, asked, "What about Rex? He quit school to be a professional bodybuilder. Then there was that creeper, Chuck, who has no business taking steroids."

"Don't worry about Rexxy. He wasn't going to graduate anyways. I would say he's dumb as dirt, but that's an insult to dirt. I don't know what to tell you about Chuck. Not many people make the hair on my neck stand up like that guy. He has "serial rapist" written all over him for sure."

That was the moment the light finally clicked in Juice's head. It didn't take as long as it did for Nolan, but they both arrived there just in the nick of time. Jared's grin went from ear to ear.

"I'm impressed with both of you. Nolan, it took you a good four months of undercover work to realize it; and Juice, it took you blabbering out loud for a few minutes to realize it; but you both did. We're not here for any glory whatsoever. In fact, you can live your life protecting the people of the world, and as soon as a cop does something wrong, the news will crucify an entire police force. We're not here for the money. We make pennies for the hours and danger we put ourselves in. We do it for the safety of our neighbors, friends, and loved ones. Sometimes along the way we lose the battle, but we don't quit fighting."

Juice stood up and wiped the tears from his eyes. "Let's go get these guys. If I know Ken, this is trial run for us."

Nolan stood up and rolled the sleeves up to his flannel shirt. "Good. We'll sell his stuff. When we come to the meeting with a thousand dollars apiece, he's going to give us more products. We'll sell that, and then we'll nail him to the wall. Might even let Gramps interrogate him and put the squeeze on who Ken answers to."

Jared clapped his hands together and rubbed them. "It's been awhile since I've made someone squirm. It's important that we stick to the plan though. Patience with this guy is the key. I know he has an airtight alibi, but I still haven't ruled him out of Cory's murder. He wasn't the guy who pulled the trigger, but he knows something about it."

Jared got up and went into the house. Nolan and Juice nodded at each other and went their separate ways. Nolan wandered up into his room and pulled out a book from his nightstand. He flipped through a few pages and stopped. His mom's journal always gave him motivation. He read the page. it was short and sweet. "Never trust anyone besides Dad.

# CHAPTER 35

Something didn't add up for Nolan. His mom was the most trusting person he'd ever met. She always gave everybody the benefit of the doubt. In fact, she and Ken probably would've hit it off and been friends if she'd ever met him. For her to put in her journal not to trust anyone besides her father made him raise an eyebrow. Nolan went down to Jared's bedroom and knocked on the door.

Nolan entered the room and sat on the foot of his grandpa's bed. He tossed the journal to his grandpa.

"Did you ever read through this after Mom died?"

"No, I didn't. I didn't even know this thing still existed. I remember she would spend hours up in her room writing in that thing. She didn't even do that when she was a teenager, so to say I was surprised would be an understatement."

"There's some interesting stuff in there," Nolan said.

"Oh yeah like what?" Jared asked.

"Most of this is about her work when she was on the force. She would jot a few thoughts down about what she did that day or if she was working on a case. Most of it is pretty boring, but toward the end, she almost becomes cynical."

"That doesn't sound like my little girl. Everything with her was rainbows, puppy dogs, and ice cream. That was her one and only fault on the force. She trusted everybody. Even the perps she arrested, she would get to know them and their stories."

"I know, that's why I came down to talk. Read the second-to-last page she wrote in."

Jared opened the book and flipped to the back. He scrunched his eyes really hard to make out the writing. He looked up, "I don't understand? Why would she only trust me? Everyone in the department loved your mom. She had more friends there than anyone."

"That's what I thought. Do you think this is why she could've been killed?"

"No, Nolan. She was murdered by a random street thug. I went over that case a thousand times, and it appears to be a case of the wrong place and the wrong time."

"But what if it wasn't?"

"I'm not going to go through that again. I spent two years trying to find the scumbag who killed her, but all it led to was disappointment and anger. I don't want to go back to that place again. I would advise that you don't go there either. You have a job to do, and trying to coldcase your mom's case isn't it."

Nolan stood up and began to leave. Before he reached the door, he turned around. "I can't believe with you and Lou on the case that Mom's killer was never arrested."

"It's my only regret. Not just my police work either. That's the only regret I've ever had in my life. I stay up at night with cold sweats knowing he's still out there. Lou and I ran down every lead, every witness, every spec of evidence, but getting away with murder is a lot easier than it should be."

Nolan leaned against the doorframe. "What do you mean?"

"Just what I said. There are some murders, when I was chief, that were as simple as tying my shoe to solve. When it was personal, they were easy. There was one case when a wife bludgeoned her husband with a cast-iron pan. She called his death in herself and said she'd been at her sister's all weekend. We called her sister, and she backed up the story, but the more we dug into the man's life, we found out about his affair with a pretty, little, blonde yoga instructor. So it was either the wife or the mistress who killed him. We brought both of them in, and the wife eventually cracked. She even told us where she buried the pan in their backyard. If they had a connection to the victim, I was going to catch them.

Then, Nolan, there are cases that can't be solved without a little luck. I remember one case where a guy was stabbed outside Northern Lumpy's bar. The guy was slumped against the fence, no witnesses, no camera, no weapon, and no DNA anywhere. We talked to the managers and owner of the bar, some people who were there that night, and a few of the waitresses. He didn't have a fight with anyone, so that theory wasn't viable. There was nothing to go on, and we were about to close the case, when the man who committed the murder came in and confessed. He said every time he saw a cop, he was sure they were coming for him. He couldn't live with it. He developed anxiety attacks, he wasn't sleeping, and he couldn't eat. His conscience got the best of him. When I asked him why he killed him, he told me he had been hired by the man's employer. He wanted to get out of paying him a bonus that he couldn't afford to give him. The employer was so cheap, he hired his neighbor to do it so that he didn't have to pay for a professional hitman. Both are in prison because the guy was a cheapskate.

Then there's your mother's murder that never gets solved. I'm reminded about my police academy sergeant telling me on the first day I was a cop that if someone wanted to get away with murder, all they had to do is pick a random person in California and open fire on them. I don't know if I buy that, but his point's well taken."

Nolan's face was whiter than rice in a snowstorm. Jared hadn't noticed this while he was telling him about the cases. "Are you okay, son?"

"I'll be fine. I'm shocked that people can be so cruel in this world. I expect that kind of behavior from crime bosses or street thugs, but the guy who would've gotten away with murder because he didn't want to pay his employee a bonus is bone-chilling. If he had hired a real hit man, no one would ever know his secret."

"That's life as a cop, Nolan. It's your job to ask the right questions and find the evidence. If you don't, then you'll have nightmares like I do."

Nolan nodded his head and left the room. He went back up to his bedroom and dumped his bag of steroids on his bed. He studied them. What were the questions he needed to ask Ken to get to his supplier? Every criminal had a secret that they were just dying to let out, and Nolan needed to find out what Ken's was.

Juice didn't know Ken well enough to know what it would be. Ken didn't trust Nolan enough to let him in on it. The only other person that might have an idea was murdered in a hotel room. Nolan went and grabbed a piece of cake that his grandpa bought from the store. He did his best thinking when sugar was involved. He made the decision to quit college and become a cop when he was drinking a milkshake. His grandpa was probably going to give him a beating for stealing his cake, but if it helped Nolan with the case, he would forgive him sooner or later.

He finished his cake and wasn't any closer to asking the right question. He saw some frosting he left on the plate. He took his index finger and swiped it across the plate to get all of the leftover frosting. As he was doing that, he remembered Rex doing the exact same thing at Karen's house during the Homecoming dinner. Nolan remembered thinking at the time that Rex was a slob, but he's tickled that Rex was. They had dinner at Coach Porter's house. Ken was on Coach Porter's staff and, by all accounts, looked up to him.

Nolan grabbed his phone from his pocket and shot Karen a text. "What personal information does your dad know about Ken?"

She replied, "What kind of personal information?"

"Anything."

"I don't know? I'll talk to Daddy."

# CHAPTER 36

*T*he road of being an undercover cop and the road to becoming a drug dealer were surprisingly similar. As a police officer trying to deceive a drug dealer, your number one priority is to have your identity never come out. Nolan got that same feeling when he sold steroids. He didn't want any of his clients to know who or where he came from. He did a lot of sneaking around as an undercover and as a drug dealer. If it wasn't for the fact that selling drugs were illegal, Nolan might have considered quitting the force for an easier and better paying job in the sales world.

Nolan went old school when the roiders wanted more juice. He had a pager and a code. When someone wanted a big order, "911" came across. They had to want at least three cycles if they put that code in though. Other times if he got a small number like six, it meant that's how many shots they wanted. The code "411" was for someone, usually a first-timer, who wanted some information on the product. Nolan was shocked by how many first-time users contacted him. Word-of-mouth business was great for him, but he had the itch to bring Ken down as soon as possible.

Nolan drove around the slums of his city. When he was growing up there, he thought it was a special place. He didn't know it had a darker part. Buildings were tagged with gang graffiti, bricks decomposed on the sides of buildings, boards were up in place of windows, and the streets were littered with trash everywhere. Nolan looked down at the address and double-checked to make sure he was at the right place.

He cautiously walked up and knocked on the door. Bars on the windows, mail piled up in front of the door, and pit bulls in the front made Nolan clench his gun inside his pocket. The door flung open, and Ken stood in the doorframe.

Nolan took a few steps back and took his hand out of his pocket. "What the hell are you doing here?" Nolan asked.

"I paged you to meet me here."

"No shit. But why? We could've met anywhere else. Your place, my place, the school . . . anywhere would've been better than this hellhole."

"Maybe, but it doesn't matter. I like this place. Most of the time when I have a new soldier meet a client here, they don't show up. In fact, the first time I met Juice here, I saw him drive around the block three times. To his credit, he manned up and came in. That's how I know I got a keeper in you, Nolan. You pulled up and knocked right on the door." Ken pointed at Nolan's pants. "I assume you got some heat in that pocket though. I saw you put your hand in there before you knocked."

"You're a bit of a Peeping Tom, I see. What the hell am I doing here, Ken?"

"You know, Juice was spot on about you. You don't listen very well. I know you heard the words coming out of my mouth, but you can't put two and two together."

Nolan began rubbing his chin. He liked the way his new prickly whiskers felt on his hands. He decided he was going to grow a beard now that he wasn't in school. He kept rubbing and scratching it when the proverbial light bulb went off. "So you bring new employees here to see if they have the stones to come up and knock on the door?"

"That's right. Now why don't you toss me your piece, and we can proceed with our meeting."

Nolan took his Glock out of his pocket and clicked out the round in the chamber. "I won't have any ammo in the chamber, but I'm not giving you my gun."

Ken lifted his shirt and showed his nine-millimeter Luger. "If you keep yours out, I'll keep mine out." Ken put his gun on the coffee table. "Why don't you at least put it on the table? My gun is lonely."

Nolan placed his gun strategically on the table, barrel facing Ken, handle close to the edge just in case he had to reach for it. Ken sat in a pee-stained, green love seat.

"You've turned into quite the little salesman. In the two weeks you've been dealing for me, you've sold more vitamin S than anybody has in their first two weeks."

Nolan reached into his pocket and flicked a few more hundred-dollar bills toward Ken. "Here's some more. I'm all about making that cash."

"You're only in it for the money? I thought you were trying to make the world a better place one muscle at a time."

Nolan laughed. "I think you have me confused with Juice."

"How is old Juice hanging in there? I haven't been able to get a hold of him for a couple of days. I have another shipment for him, and we need to get it out on the streets before too long."

"You have more drugs for him? He hasn't been able to unload the merchandise you gave him last week. It's still hanging out in the gym bags at my grandpa's house."

Ken stood up and kicked the coffee table that had the guns on them. The guns flew toward Nolan. He jumped out of his seat and ducked behind the couch. "What the hell, Ken? Those guns have live ammo in them."

"We both took the bullets out of our chambers. Quit being such a candy-ass," Ken said.

"If avoiding getting shot by a stray bullet makes me a candy-ass, then consider my ass covered in chocolate and nougat."

Ken plopped down hard on the chair. This time dust particles flew everywhere. "I need to get that moved. Cory may have been a crybaby punk, but at least he did what I told him to. Juice and his newfound love of school is going to put a lot of us in a bind that we may not be able to fix."

"Unless you have a mouse in your pocket, you better not say we. This is between you and Juice. I do my work."

Ken sat up straight. "That's where you're wrong. If one of us in the Red Rock crew comes up short, we all come up short. Trying to explain to our boss that we came up short this week is going to get one of us real familiar with worms."

Nolan stood stoic. "If this guy wants to come at me for a few dollars, then he will have to realize he's fighting for his life as well."

"Do you really think he cares if he's in a fight for his life? I'm pretty sure he thrives on that type of fight. He terrifies me. He's the type of guy who is well respected, but he has some serious ghosts in his closet." Ken shivered. "He brags all the time about torturing his partner . . . pulling his fingernails off his fingers, jamming nails into his toes, putting him through the worst hell imaginable . . . then he put a bullet through his head. When he recalls that memory, he always laughs and smiles. It's like Satan is in the room with me."

"And this is the guy who gets us our drugs?" Nolan asked.

"I've seen his warehouse. He grows his own pot, cooks his own meth, and takes the profit from those and buys some of the best coke around. Then he makes a profit off of that."

Nolan had to sit back down. His brain couldn't believe what his ears were hearing. He grabbed his gun from the floor and put it back in his waistband. "How do the steroids factor into his drug ring?"

"Some doctor hooks him up or something like that. I told you, this guy's powerful, respected, and dangerous. We need to get the money from Juice, and we need to sell all this new shit." Ken pointed at three gym bags full of various types and sizes of drugs.

"I want to meet him," Nolan said.

"No way! You've been selling for two weeks. You're not even a full-time soldier, and you want to meet the commander?"

Nolan stood up and clicked a bullet into the chamber of his Glock. "If this guy is as tough as you say he is, then I'm not going to sit around and wait for him to come to me. I'm going to be proactive and let him know who I am."

Ken grabbed his gun and tapped the window with it. "He knows you. Trust me. You don't think he'd let anyone sell for him, do you?"

"Good. Set up the meeting," Nolan said.

"He's not going to meet with you."

"Then give me his number and I'll call him."

"For someone who jumped behind the couch because of a stray bullet, you sure seem to want to get yourself killed."

"It's going to be fine," Nolan said.

"Are you not hearing me? It's a suicide mission. If you go and tell him that Juice came up short, he's going to slice, shoot, or bludgeon you."

"This isn't hard, Kenny. Tell him I have the money. I want to meet him to talk about career advancement."

"What are you going to do when he finds out you're lying. If you didn't have his money, he may put a bullet through your head. When he finds out you lied to him, you're going to be begging for that bullet."

"Who says I won't have the money? Just make the call and set it up."

Nolan busted through the door and jumped into his car. He cruised down the boulevard with his windows down. St. George wasn't like the rest of Utah. It didn't have thin air. You could catch your breath there, and after the ambush Nolan set up for himself, he needed to catch his breath more than ever.

Nolan drove with the wind blowing his hair back. When he decided to go undercover, he thought he was going to catch some young potheads. He even thought he might be able to change some of these kids for the better—after getting the credit for busting them of course—but he had stumbled onto something that was much deeper. Who was this monster who would torture his own partner, and what did his partner do to anger him? Nolan knew he had to put this parasite out of commission, but he also quivered at the thought of meeting him.

# CHAPTER 37

*H*earing tires squeal around the corner, Juice looked out the living room window. These last couple of weeks living in Jared's house brought sheer joy to Juice. He was going to night school, he was getting out of the drug business, and he finally had a plan with his life. He wasn't under his stepfather's thumb, and he flourished when nobody was constantly harassing him like his mom would.

Jared was always more than willing to talk and listen with Juice. Juice never knew either of his grandpas, so having Jared around was like having one for the first time. The only thing that kept him up at night was Nolan's gung-ho attitude toward Ken. Juice had known Ken long enough to know that he didn't like being put into a corner. If Nolan pressed Ken too hard, Ken would come out firing.

Juice heard a car roaring around the corner and then watched it park in the driveway.

*That cracker sure likes to drive fast,* Juice thought. Juice walked over to the front door and opened it before Nolan was at the steps. Nolan strutted in.

"What are you so damn happy about?" Juice asked.

"Everything fell into place. It was beautiful. I didn't need to cry, beg, or steal. Ken fell right into my trap."

"Noles, what happened?"

"You should've seen it. Ken offered him up on a silver platter, and I gobbled it up. We're in."

"Quit trippin', Noles, and tell me who Ken ratted out?"

Nolan smiled and put his arm around Juice. "It all went like this. Ken was freaking out about you still having some drugs left to sell, so I convinced him to get me a meeting with his supplier. Just because we haven't exchanged the drugs for money."

Juice threw Nolan's arm off him and shoved him to the floor. "Why did you say anything about us have drugs still? You just got us smoked."

Nolan went into the kitchen and cracked open a bottle of Mountain Dew. "Not you too? Ken acted like a frightened little puppy just like you are. I'm a police officer and a former division one football player. I can handle myself, and more importantly, I can handle my gun. I had Ken set up a meeting. Are you in?"

Juice paced the kitchen and living room floor. He could've walked a 5K with as much pacing as he was doing. "From the tales I've heard, this gent ain't no one we need to screw around with."

Nolan grabbed another soda and tossed it to Juice. "I need you there, Juice. We need to show that we're a solid unit and that they can trust us to deliver the goods."

"Shouldn't you get some of your police buddies to roll with you, so they can—well, you know—arrest the criminals?"

"We're not busting them right now, we're just having a meeting. Once we meet, I'll be able to identify the supplier. Once I'm able to identify the supplier, I'll be able to report back to Lou and my grandpa. When I report back to them, they can build a case against this jerk. After they build a case against him, then they arrest him, and we get to transfer Ken to the Point of the Mountain medium security prison. It's a magnificent process."

Juice's color began to return to his face. Either Nolan was the best liar around, or he truly believed they were on the verge of something great. Juice hadn't decided what side of the fence he was on, but he knew that Nolan made convincing arguments. Juice also knew that the only way for him to purge himself of his past was to get rid of the temptations of his past. That was good enough reason for him to help Nolan see this thing to the end.

"Okay, Noles. I'll roll with you to the meet-and-greet, but I think we need to exchange those drugs for some cash real quick. I don't want to go into the meeting with this psychopath ready to exterminate me."

Nolan nodded his head. "I couldn't agree more. There's one tiny complication to that though."

Juice zipped up his jacket. "Oh yeah, what's that?"

"Lou said he wasn't going to give us any more money for drugs. He said we should have plenty of evidence to put Ken away."

Juice unzipped his jacket and put it back on the coat rack. "That's more than a tiny complication. That's an iceberg-taking-the-Titanic-out problem, Noles. How are we supposed to get the cheddar for these drugs?"

Nolan handed Juice a cell phone. "I think you already know the answer to that question. Make some appointments. We need to unload . . . and quick."

Juice threw the phone back at him. "No! I promised Jared that that life was gone. I'm not slinging no more. I'm going to get my GED, and I'm becoming a cop. A good cop, not no crooked asshole like yourself. You're a wolf in sheep's clothes. You want to get to the supplier so bad you can't even see that we have Ken all ready to bust. No, you want to get a bigger fish, so you'll compromise yourself and your gramps to get the bigger bust. And all for what, so Lou can pat your head and tell you you're a good boy? And the whole time you haven't realized all Lou really wants is for you to bust Ken and get the shit out of the schools?"

Nolan played with his new goatee. He pinched the hair in between his thumb and index finger. "I know what Lou wants. I also know he can't see the forest through the trees. He's nowhere close to solving Cory's murder; and he was the lead detective on my mom's murder, and he came up with nothing. I know what Lou wants, and it's bullshit. He wants another arrest to make his record appear great; but when it comes to down to it, he's a small-time police chief. Wyatt Earp, Bufford Pusser, Pat Garret, all those guys are difference-makers in this world. When bad things happened under their watch, they kicked ass. They have movies and books written about them. If you're not striving to be like them as a cop, then what are you even in this business for?"

266

Juice pleaded with Nolan. "Those guys didn't become cops to become famous. They just happened to do their jobs. If you're a cop to become famous, then you need to bounce off the force. You need to do the job that's in front of you."

"Maybe if you had any type of education, you would know who those sheriffs were. Then you would have an appreciation of what I'm trying to do."

Juice plopped on the living room couch and sighed. "I never thought you would play the dumb card on me, Noles. I may not have a formal education like a lot of smarter people, but I'm not sure you know why those sheriffs are famous."

Nolan sat down across the room from Juice. "How so?"

"Wyatt Earp was a peace keeper. That old boy didn't hardly ever squeeze that trigger. And Bufford Pusser fought a war on gambling and moonshine to protect his hometown. Then you want to talk about Pat Garret? He chased down Billy the Kid! Billy Boney, for hell's sake, was one of America's most famous outlaws. He killed men left and right. So if you want to run down ole Billy the Kid, then I got your back. Until then, let's arrest Ken. Play it safe, and make a case on the boss another time."

Nolan's eyes impaled Juice's soul. "You've heard the stories about this maniac. So I'm going after him. He may not have killed as many men as Billy the Kid, but he's just as dangerous. I'm taking him down, and I need your help. Pick up the phone and make the calls. We need some cash."

Juice slowly reached for the phone. He scrolled down his contact list and found a number. He dialed it and waited. "Uncle Rob. You got need for weed, and I need some quick cash."

Rob agreed to meet Nolan and Juice at a truck stop halfway between Mesquite and St. George. It was a half-hour drive for Nolan and Juice, so they snagged their drugs and bolted in Juice's Camaro.

They slipped into the back of the truck stop and parked in the darkness. A few truckers were inside the gas station lounging on an unexpectedly nice leather couch watching the sixty-inch flat screen. Some sitcom was on, and no one noticed Juice and Nolan when they tiptoed in. Juice went to the restaurant that was inside the gas station and sat at a booth next to the window. He examined to road leading into the stop and kept fidgeting in the booth.

A young, blonde, very pretty waitress—who looked like she was in need of a sandwich—came up to his table. "Want to look at a menu?"

"No thanks. I'm not here to eat," Juice said.

The waitress slid in to the booth next to Juice. "Oh, so you're here for something other than food?"

"Yeah, something like that."

The waitress leaned into Juice and whispered in his ear. "I go for a hundred dollars a night. If that's too rich for your blood, there is Jenny in the back. She can usually be haggled down to fifty."

Juice smiled and calmly said, "I appreciate the offer, and you're a gorgeous girl, but that guy I came in with," Juice pointed over at Nolan who was watching television with the truckers, "he's actually a cop, and I'm not sure he'd be cool with me paying for sex tonight. I will take a cup of coffee though." The waitress winked at Juice and poured him a cup.

"So that goofy, white bread, corn fed, egomaniac really is a cop." Juice turned his head over his shoulder, and there was Uncle Rob, dressed to impress as always. Snakeskin shoes, silk tie, and a yellow pinstriped suit, with a black vest and hat to match.

"Uncle, I've never seen you look as much as a pimp as you do right now. What's with the yellow suit?"

Rob brushed his hands on his suit jacket as if brushing off dirt. "Ah, you know how it is, nephew. This is one of the first suits I ever owned. Cost me 250 dollars. I used to strut around in this thing fifteen years ago."

"So why are you wearing it tonight?" Juice asked.

"The little, old Asian lady closed down her dry cleaning next to my casino, and I haven't found anyone to clean my suits yet. I remember one time I had a drunk throw up all over one of my shirts at the casino. Man, I thought that funk would never leave my shirt; but I took it to her the next morning, and presto, she had that shirt smelling like a bed of roses on a spring morning. Ever since then, I took all my clothes to her. Now I don't know what to do. Everything I own is dirty."

"Why don't you go to another dry cleaner?"

"Not an option, young blood. I can't go back to eating ham sandwiches once I've experienced prime rib." Rob sat down across from Juice and put his hat in the middle of the table.

Juice slid the keys to his Camaro to his uncle. "In the trunk of my car, you'll find close to ten pounds of top quality purple kush. I'll take five thousand for both bricks."

Rob slid the key back to Juice. "Why are we making a deal for drugs with your cop buddy right there?"

"Because it was his idea to sell it."

Rob grinned and took the handkerchief out of his front pocket and wiped the sweat off his forehead. "You got him on the take, don't you? I knew you always had your daddy's smarts. It's too bad your mom left him for that jerk off of a judge."

"Thanks, Uncle. You know how I always looked up to you, so that means a lot coming from you."

"You know I love you, young nephew, but five thousand dollars for ten pounds is too much. I won't make any money off of it."

One thing about Rob that Juice knew for certain was that he was the best negotiator he'd been around. Juice needed, at bare minimum, two thousand; and getting that from Rob was going to be close to impossible. Not only was Rob a great negotiator, he also knew how much pot went for. He could get a little more for it in Nevada. Desperate gamblers in need of a quick pick-me-up made Rob a lot of money over the years. That was Juice's only saving grace.

Juice's voice cracked. "What's your top dollar for everything?" Juice gave Rob a gaze that mirrored a puppy leaving his mom for the first time.

The look didn't faze Rob. "I'll give you fifteen hundred. Final offer."

Juice was stuck. He couldn't take the deal, but he needed to get some money out of Rob. He knew Rob wasn't going to budge from the fifteen hundred unless something drastic changed. Juice was about to accept the offer and roll the dice with Ken and the supplier when Nolan came over and slid in next to Rob.

"Rob, it's good to see you. How's everything?" Nolan asked.

Rob grabbed his hat and put it back on. "This is a meeting between my nephew and me. I don't recall ordering a plate of bacon."

"You're a funny guy. It's because I'm a cop. I get it. Seriously though, we're going to need at least double of your offer, and we're going to need it tonight."

Rob tried to force his way out of the booth, but Nolan held firm and didn't let him squirm his way out.

"Okay, I see you got some courage all of a sudden," Rob said. "I'll tell you what. How about I give you a thousand, and I won't have my associate outside bash your face in."

Rob pointed toward his security guard. It was the same man that Juice and Nolan met at the casino the first time Nolan met Rob. Nolan studied the man through the window. He still looked like he could bench-press a car, but he was clean-shaven this time. He looked more professional, and a little bit scarier.

"That's a good deal, Rob, "Nolan said, "but let me make one counter and see if you like it." By this time, Nolan had to force his confidence and speak in a deeper voice. He didn't want to talk tough and have his voice crack like a pubescent teenager. He put his hands in his pockets so Rob couldn't see them shake. "You crossed the Arizona-Utah border. Now, if we would've met in Nevada or Arizona, you would've had the upper hand. But since we're in Washington County, Utah, I still have jurisdiction. So here's what I propose: you give me three thousand, you take the drugs, and you never hear from me again. If you don't take the offer, I arrest you and your muscle for buying drugs from Juice, and I get the Mesquite PD to look into your prostitution ring."

Rob wiggled and played around with his suit. "You can't arrest me for buying drugs when you're the seller. It will never stand up in court."

"I don't need it to stand up in court. I just need you in jail for the night. We're only thirty minutes from your casino, and with you in jail, I could clean the place out."

Rob looked at Juice and shook his head. "Damn, nephew. What kind of crooked, crazy criminal did you get mixed up with?"

Juice slid the keys to Rob one more time. "You think I have him on the take? Well it's the exact opposite; he has me by the balls in a vice grip."

Rob grabbed the key and gave Nolan an envelope full of cash. "There's twenty-five hundred dollars in there. That's all you're getting."

Juice yanked the envelope from Nolan's hands before he could say anything. "We'll take it, Uncle. Thank you. You have no idea how much I needed this. It's a literal life saver."

"Rob stood up and straightened his vest. "Don't let this pig get you mixed up in something you can't handle. Keep your head on straight, nephew." Rob looked at Nolan. "Next time I see you, I'm taking my damn shoes back. To think I felt sorry for you the first time I met you. You're nothing but a hustler with a badge."

"There isn't going to be a next time, Rob. All you need to do is stay in Nevada, and I won't ever come across your path again."

Rob left the gas station. Nolan watched Rob open the trunk to Juice's car. He took the drugs and handed them to his bodyguard. They got in Rob's black Escalade, and two red tail lights pulled away. Juice stood up and kicked open the truck stop's doors. Nolan sheepishly grinned, put a five-dollar bill on the table, and followed him out to the car.

# CHAPTER 38

*T*he drive home would've made Jeff Gordon proud. Juice put the pedal to the floor and didn't let up until they pulled into St. George. Juice fishtailed into a fast food parking lot. He parked the car and flung the door open. He went and sat on the hood of his car. Nolan went out and stood across him with his arms folded.

"I know you're pissed off, but I did what I had to do to get us our money. I needed that money tonight. I didn't have time to play Rob's games."

Juice jumped down from the car. "You don't treat family that way. I would've gotten the money without being an ass."

"Would you have? Whenever you get around your Uncle Rob, he completely owns you. You don't have the fortitude to do business with him. He would've walked out of there with the drugs for fifteen hundred dollars and would've been screwed to the wall."

"I don't see it that way. My relationship with my uncle is one of mutual respect. I told him you were a cop. He loves me, so he wouldn't have low-balled me. I give him information, and he gives me fair rates. It's been that way since I was thirteen."

Nolan put his hand over his face and shook his head. "Listen to you. He's been taking advantage of you since before puberty. And you're so loyal to him, you haven't been able to see what's right in front of your face, or you don't realize you're just another buster to him. Either way, we weren't leaving that truck stop without the amount of cash that I needed."

"Why did you need the money tonight? I thought the plan was to get what we could from Rob and get the rest from Lou."

"We don't have time to see Lou tonight. I got a text from Ken while we were at the truck stop. We have a meeting with the distributor in about two hours."

Juice pulled the envelope full of hundreds out of his inside jacket pocket and flopped it down on the car. "You got what you needed. Let's go make that bust then."

They got back into the car and drove to Jared's house. Jared was waiting for them in the driveway.

"How'd the meeting with Rob go?"

Nolan took out the envelope and handed it to Jared. "We got what we needed. I need to go change clothes, maybe take a quick shower. I'll see you in a few minutes."

Jared looked at Juice and sighed. "We'll see him in an hour. That kid sure does love to primp."

Juice gave a half-smile and nodded.

"What's wrong, Juice?"

"It's that crazy-ass grandson of yours. The way he treated my uncle was insulting."

276

"What'd he do?" Jared asked.

"He treated him like a criminal. He says that my uncle takes advantage of me, but I don't think he does. We've done business together for a long time. He's the only link I have to my dad."

Jared tapped his fingertips together. "I get where you're coming from, Juice, but I'm going to tell you something you may not want to hear. Your Uncle Rob is a common criminal. He's a drug-dealing, flesh-pedaling, crooked casino boss. I've never met the guy, so I can't comment on your relationship with him. I made a career of catching people like your uncle my entire life, and I am fairly certain he is taking advantage of you. With that being said, Nolan is an abrasive, ignorant little weasel at times. But I think you know that he's changed since the first time you met him. He was on the verge of getting fired from the police force for being a know-it-all who couldn't take direct orders to someone who's about to crack the biggest drug case in Southern Utah. And you need to take pride in knowing you played a huge role in that."

A real smile finally crept across Juice's face. "He still needs to take direction better."

Jared smirked. "Some things are never going to change with that kid."

"Ain't that the truth?"

Jared turned to go inside but then he stopped and paused. "Does Nolan have a date with Karen tonight?"

"Not that I know of. Why?"

"How come he's inside getting ready at 8:00 p.m.?"

"We got a meeting with the big boy tonight. Ken set the whole thing up."

Jared's hands began to shake, and he couldn't control them. "You have a meeting tonight?" Jared ran to the front door and stuck his head inside it and screamed, "Nolan get your butt down in the living room right now." He gestured for Juice to get inside. Juice went in and sat on the loveseat.

Nolan came down the stairs in red gym shorts still wet from his shower. "Where's the fire, Grandpa?"

"It's going to be in the meeting you have tonight."

"Is that what's bothering you? Don't sweat it. Tonight's a meet-and-greet. I'm going to give him the money, identify our mystery drug lord, and report back to Lou. I'm not going to arrest anybody by myself tonight."

Jared stood up and patrolled back and forth in the living room. "I don't like it. Not without any backup. Nothing good happens when you're by yourself."

Nolan glanced over at Juice. "I won't be by myself. I've got Juice."

"No. You're not taking Juice. He's doesn't have the training to handle a situation like this."

Nolan cracked up. "Who is more qualified to handle this than Juice? One of the unis down at the station? They would piss themselves the second drugs and money were brought out. I trust Juice with my life. He knows these streets and this world better than anyone. If we try to set up an ambush, were as good as dead. We don't have the time or resources to get everyone into place."

Juice zipped up his jacket. "Jared, with all due respect, I know where the meeting's at, and I know Ken. I don't really need your permission to go. I got Noles' back no matter what goes down tonight. I've been part of too many of these little meetings with Ken. He's not going to do anything. He doesn't have the stones."

Jared held his breath for a long pause then exhaled. "Ken's not the problem. It's the man he answers to that scares me."

Juice and Nolan shared a glance. "Yeah, he frightens all of us," Nolan said.

Nolan went back up to his room. He opened his mom's journal and read one of her entries. He looked at the date. It was four days before her murder.

*I cannot begin to tell you about the day I had today. I know that my dad is under a lot of stress, but he really needs to take this drug cartel forming in St. George seriously. Whenever I bring it up, he brushes it to the side and tells me to get back to the robbery investigations. I know there have been a slew of break-ins, but any rookie can take the lead on that. When I bring it up to Lou, he laughs in my face. He thinks street punks on dope, as he puts it, aren't anything to get my panties in a wad about.*

*The sexist nature at that place is overwhelming. I have to work twice as hard and still have to put up with their remarks. I'll tell you what though. When I crack this drug case without any of their help, I'm going to take over as the police chief when Dad retires. When that day comes, I'll make sure that Lou's panties are completely bunched.*

*Enough about work though. I could go on for pages, but my hand couldn't take anymore marathon journal entries. But I love the fact that Nolan is going to be a college man. I don't want him to walk a beat. He needs to keep his sweet smile. Working the streets can change anyone, and Nolan is too good for this. I can't wait for his college graduation. I'll push him towards law school, but that can wait.*

Nolan put the journal down and gazed over at his gun and badge. *Law school,* he thought. *That's interesting.* He always wanted to be a cop, and he thought that's what his mom wanted, as well. The clock read 9:45. He had fifteen minutes until the meeting, and he needed to get his mind right. He took his mom's journal and stuffed it in his backpack. He grabbed his gun and his backup, just in case. He tucked one in his waistband and the other in the front pocket of his pack.

He went down and knocked on Juice's door. He opened it before Juice could say anything and poked his head in. "You ready man?"

Juice got up off his cot and grabbed his gun. "Yeah, let's go."

"Do you really think you should be carrying? If something goes down and you shoot someone, I may have to arrest you."

"If it gets to the point where I may need to pop someone, I'd rather take my chances with a lawyer mom and judge stepfather than with the nut job shooting at me."

Nolan nodded. "Alright, let's go. Let's take your car."

Juice snatched his keys off the dresser and followed Nolan upstairs. They got in the car and revved it up. "You got the address, Noles?"

"Yeah, 294 East Road 19."

"I know that place. It's not the first time Ken has held a pow-wow there."

"Do you know the lay of the land there?"

"A little bit. They'll be waiting in the alley between two abandoned warehouses. Only one way in and out, and they'll have us surrounded for sure."

"That's good. If they want to get out, they have to come through us."

"I'm not so sure that's a good thing," Juice said.

They crept up to the address. As Nolan expected, it was back in the rundown part of town. The two cold metal warehouses had broken windows from rocks being thrown through them. Juice crept his car to the opening of the front of the alley. Ken stood tall at the top of the boxes that were piled up in a pyramid shape. He looked like he thought he was the king of the shithole.

Nolan grabbed the cash and put it in his pants pocket. He turned to Juice. "Stay in the car. I'll call you out when the time is right."

Juice nodded his head. Although, he did pull his piece out and placed it on his lap. Nolan got out of the car and took a few steps toward Ken. "Stop right there, young man. Why isn't Juice getting out? Juice and I go way back. Is he trying to hurt my feelings?"

"I told him to stay in the car. This doesn't concern him. I sold his drugs, and I got the money. I don't need him getting any credit for my sales."

"Alright Nolan, I like that kind of grit. Where's the money?"

Nolan held up the white envelope. "Why don't you come down here and get it?"

"Okay." Ken jumped down form the top of the box pyramid and went over to Nolan. He held his hand out, and Nolan gave him the money. Ken opened the envelope and pulled out the cash. He flipped it through his fingers. "How did you get this kind of cash that quick?"

"I know a guy in Nevada. He took two bricks off of me. I'm sure he'll just end up selling it at a higher rate, but that's not my headache."

"You're right; that's not yours. But it could very well be mine. You see, if you're selling our stuff for someone else to sell, then I have to be the one who explains to L why his drugs are being sold for a higher profit and why he's not getting a piece of that pie."

Nolan burst out laughing. "The big bad man's name is L? That's the least manly name I've ever heard. Pablo Escobar, that name screams drug king. L screams, 'I'm a teenage dancer.'"

"That's his name, so if you want to make fun of it to his face, then be my guest. However, if you do, he's going to break your legs."

"I would love to make fun of him to his face. Where is he?"

Juice was eavesdropping on the conversation and feared Nolan sounded more like a cop at this point than a dealer who wanted to impress the boss. He slid out the window and went up and shook Ken's hand.

"Juice, how could you let this newb take your drugs and get the money for him. There was a time nobody could bring in what you could?"

Juice threw his hands up. "I must be slipping."

Ken examined Juice up and down. "Nah, that's not it. There's something different about you. I know what it is. You're actually trying to get an education."

"Oh yeah, who told you that?"

"Nobody told me. Did you forget I'm getting my teaching license? I see you on campus every Monday and Wednesday night. That's when they teach their GED class, right?"

"Yep, I figured if this job didn't work out for me, I would at least have a GED so I could get into some type of trade school."

"You two can compare class schedules some other time." Nolan walked towards the boxes a few steps. "But for now, can I meet the man I came here to meet?"

Ken glanced in Juice's direction. "Can you believe this guy? The first time I met him, he was made a fool by that lard-ass Bitton. You should've seen him, Juice. He wandered the hallways looking for a classroom that didn't exist. When I was having a bad day, I would think back to that day, and it would make me laugh out loud. Now he's giving me orders. I'm so proud of my little man growing up."

Juice cracked a smile. "Yeah, the first time I met this clown, he tried to keep up with me in the weight room. You should've seen his chicken legs trying to squat."

Nolan shot Juice a death stare. It was one thing for Ken to be mocking him, but he thought Juice was there to back him up.

"If you two want to take a trip down memory lane, even though it wasn't that long ago, can you do it some other time? You told me that L was going to be here. I need to talk with him."

Ken pulled a baseball hat out of his back pocket. The brim was almost folded in half. It looked like it was white at one point, but now it was a dirt- and sweat-stained mess. He examined it then put it on. "My first Red Rock High baseball hat holds a special place in my heart. The hours of dedication I put into trying to be the next great baseball star . . . I used to go out to my backyard and pretend to be Ken Griffey, Jr. I would be in the bottom of the ninth, bases loaded, down by three runs. Greg Maddox would throw me a back door slider, and I would swing that sweet swing. Crack! I would hit it out of the park, and I would do my homerun trot around the basses. Great times."

Juice and Nolan shared a jumbled look. "Yeah, I used to do the same thing in my driveway, except I was Magic Johnson winning the finals," Juice said.

"I did the same thing. What does any of this have to do with the meeting?" Nolan asked.

Ken pulled his hat down almost over his eyes. He had to tilt his chin up to see. "I used to play shortstop with my hat like this. I made an error in the state championship game my sophomore year. Coach blamed my hat for it, but it was my nerves. They got the best of me. I read the ball off the bat. and got my glove down. The ball hit off the heel of my glove, and I booted it. It had nothing to do with my vision, but coach was adamant about me not being able to see the ball. Ironically enough, it was his tunnel vision that got him fired a few years later."

Nolan nodded. "I remember that coach. Didn't he get fired for starting his son over Kade McGee in the region championship?"

"That's him. Kade went on to become a minor league pitcher, and his boy struggled to find a junior college to give him a shot. That's not really the point of the story."

Juice pointed at his wrist as if to mimic a watch. "Well, do you want to get to the point?"

"How long have you been dealing for me, Juice?" Ken asked.

"I don't know, about two years?"

"Two years and you've never asked to meet L. You've been a good soldier. You've always come through for us. I've been selling since that game my sophomore year. I was looking for an advantage and knew a guy who sold steroids. Long story short, instead of taking the steroids, I decided to distribute them and make some money. That was eight years ago. I met L last year. I worked my way up for seven years before I could even meet with him." Ken turned and gawked at Nolan. "You want to meet him after a couple of good weeks. Something didn't sit right with me. I went back and forth on why you wanted this meeting. Were you the universe's most aggressive drug dealer, or were you a cop?"

Nolan opened the driver's side door of the Camaro and stood next to it, one hand on the door, one foot inside the car. "We've had this conversation before. You accuse me of being a cop once, that's fine. You're doing your due diligence. But I don't need this job. I don't want to have this conversation with you every time I request something. Screw you and L. I'm going home."

Nolan waved for Juice to get into the car. He shut the driver's side door when he heard a loud noise that ripped through his eardrums. Bang-Bang! He grabbed his ears as they pierced with ringing. He barely got a glance of Ken bolting away from the alley. He rubbed his eyes and noticed Juice lying in front of the car. Nolan smashed out of the car and slid next to Juice. Blood flowed out of the bullet holes.

Nolan slapped his face. "Juice, wake up, damn it. You need to wake up. You're going to be a hell of a cop, but you need to wake up."

# CHAPTER 39

Nolan stood over Juice's limp body. He grabbed Juice and struggled, dragging him over to his car. Nolan grabbed the radio out of his backpack and screamed in it, "Get a bus here immediately. Gunshot wound to the chest, and the victim doesn't have a pulse. I'm starting CPR." Nolan started compressions to Juice's chest, but on every compression, blood shot out of Juice's bullet wound. If Nolan kept this up, Juice would bleed out before the ambulance arrived. Nolan took off his shirt and applied pressure to the wound. He leaned in to Juice and whispered, "I'm sorry. I'm so sorry."

He waited for what felt like an eternity for the ambulance to arrive. When it finally did, Nolan explained what had happened and how Ken was still out there. The EMT did his examination on Juice. Nolan, standing over his shoulder, just kept saying, "Come on, Juice, fight it. You're too strong to let this asshole win."

After a few minutes of trying to get Juice stabilized, the EMT looked over at Nolan and said, "You better call in the detectives. This just turned into a homicide."

Juice was dead. Nolan ran to Juice's car and fired the V8 up. The squeal of the tires, the engine roaring, and the nitrous burning, Nolan flew out of the alley. He didn't know where he was going, and he didn't know what he was going to do when he got there, but the gates of hell weren't going to stop Nolan from getting Ken.

He took out his phone and dialed Karen.

"Hello?"

"Karen, I need you to think really hard. Where would Ken go if he were trying to hide?"

"How would I know?" Karen mumbled, still groggy and trying to wake up.

Nolan's cracking voice spit out, "I thought your dad and Ken were close?"

"Not really. Ken just works for Dad. I don't know if they even talk outside of coaching?"

"Karen, I just pulled up to your house; let me in."

Nolan waited for Karen to let him in. He didn't know how he was going to tell her that Juice was dead or that he was an undercover cop. The door swung open and Nolan bear-hugged Karen.

"What the hell, Nolan? Why is there blood all over you?"

"Go get your dad."

Karen ran upstairs and grabbed her Dad. Coach Porter hobbled down the stairs and to the living room where Nolan waited. Nolan stood up and shook the coaches' hand.

"Sir, I need your help."

"What's going on? Are you in some kind of trouble?" Porter rubbed his eyes.

"Not me. It's Ken."

"Ken? What kind of trouble?"

"He's a drug dealer, and he just murdered Juice."

Karen and Coach Porter both turned white as snow. Karen began to bawl. Nolan tried to put his arm around her and comfort her, but she couldn't stop. She sunk her head into Nolan's chest and continued to sob.

"How do you know all this?" Coach Porter asked.

"I was there when it happened," Nolan said.

Karen stopped crying long enough to ask, "What were you doing there?"

"I needed some evidence to make an arrest."

"I see," Coach Porter said in a very deep voice. "It looks like you're not who you say you are."

"Daddy, what are you talking about? I don't understand what the hell is going on?" Karen said.

"That's true, Rocco. I'm not who I say I am." Nolan lifted Karen's head out of his chest. He looked her in the eyes. He loved those eyes. "Karen, since the first day I met you, I've been a cop. I was sent in by Principal Bitton to find out where all the drugs have been coming from. None of that is important right now. Juice is dead. I watched Ken shoot him, and now I need your help."

Coach Porter looked at Nolan and said, "Ken's dad has an old ranch that his family uses to raise cattle. He's always talking about it. If Ken were to hide out, that would be my best guess. It's in Fillmore City."

"Fillmore? That's has to be 150 miles north. He has an hour head start, so he's almost there." Nolan ran out the door and jumped into Juice's car. He looked out the window to see Karen standing on the front porch. He stuck his head out the window. "When I started this assignment, my only goal was to make the bust and become relevant in my department. Meeting you beats any goals I could've set for myself."

Karen smiled. "How old are you? Anything over thirty and were going to have a problem."

"We'll be alright then."

Nolan sped off and headed toward I-15 North. He called Lou and told him where he was going and that he needed backup. Nolan raced at speeds over one hundred miles per hour reflecting on what had just happened. *Why did Ken shoot Juice? Only three people in the world knew that Juice was a CI, and Ken sure as hell wasn't one of them.* He slammed on the breaks and pulled over to the side of the road. "That rat scum bastard!" he shouted inside the car.

# CHAPTER 40

*E*verybody in the police station headed toward
Fillmore, but Nolan was going back to St. George.
He pulled up behind a big oak tree so he would be hidden
from the view. He looked into the window. He saw Ken
sitting at a desk slowly sipping bourbon. Ken slumped
in the chair, and he could hardly keep his eyes open. He
even nodded off a couple of times.

Nolan got out of the car and snuck around the
back. He looked around at the best place to sneak in.
He thought maybe the second story window, but there
wasn't anything for him to shimmy up to get that high.
Maybe he could try and pick one of the locks to the door?
He had two options. He could try and sneak in and be
silent, but Nolan's two left feet made it impossible to be
quiet, or he could arrive with a bang. He needed some
help if he was going to do this. He raced back to the car
and made a quick phone call.

"I need your help, Grandpa!"

"Up in Fillmore?" Jared asked.

"How'd you know I was going to Fillmore?"

"Lou called. He told me you broke the case open. He wanted me to surprise you up there after your first big arrest."

"Don't go up to Fillmore. Meet me at Lou's house. He's the guy. He's the boss. Ken kept calling him L. It's his damn initial, L.

Nolan hung up the phone. He walked up the steps to the house and kicked open the door. He darted toward the kitchen and swung the door wide open. Ken sprung out of his seat and spilled his drink all over. Ken reached for his gun on the table, but Nolan had cut him off at the pass.

"How'd you know I was a cop? You had me figured out. I just want to know how."

"I'm pretty sure you already know. If you didn't, then you wouldn't have come here. Lou sold you out. Why couldn't you just bust Cory? If you did the simple thing like bust Cory, he and Juice would still be alive."

"Where is Lou? I know he's around here somewhere." Nolan scanned the room to make sure he wasn't missing anything.

"Come on out, you piece of trash!" Nolan screamed at the top of his lungs. Lou was nowhere to be found.

"Did you think that would actually work?" Ken chuckled a little bit. "Hey, come out so I can arrest you. I'm shocked he didn't come out."

"When you're right, you're right, Ken. I guess I'll have to settle by bringing you in for murder two. Does twenty-five to life sound good to you?"

"Hold on. I didn't kill anyone."

"Bullshit, Ken. I was there. I saw you in the alley. How stupid do you think I am?"

"You saw Juice get shot. Not by me. No way am I taking the rap for that."

Nolan notice a shadow creeping around the corner. He turned with his gun pointed. Lou came into the room.

"Just in time for the party," Nolan said. "Ken, here, is going away for murder, and was about to concoct a story about how he didn't do it."

"Let's let him talk just for fun," Lou said in a serious tone. "Well Kenny, my boy, let's hear this tall tale of murder."

"You can hear it through my lawyer," Ken answered back viciously.

"Enough of this!" Nolan screamed. "Put your hands over your head, Lou. I'm taking both of you in."

Lou sat at the kitchen table next to Ken. "No you're not. First off, nobody is going to believe you. You don't have anything. All you have is a person you saw kill Juice tell you that I sold you out. That's not exactly solid evidence."

Nolan sat down at the table next to them. He knocked on the table legs. "I remember your love for woodwork. You like to make fancy wood furniture with hollow hiding spots. I thought that was kind of mysterious, but it makes sense know. Where else would you hide your drugs? I called some backup, and we're going to search this place. My best guess is we're going to find all sorts of narcotics. After that, I'll have more than enough to drag your sorry butt to jail."

293

Lou put his elbows on the table. "I guess when you're licked there's nothing to do but surrender. Or maybe you can look over your right shoulder."

Nolan looked, but there wasn't anyone there. He turned back toward Lou. Lou pulled out his pistol and hit Nolan on the head with the butt of his gun. Nolan crumpled and fell like a bag of bricks out of his chair. Lou turned and punched Ken in the face. Ken fell to the ground and got back up rubbing his cheek.

"Are you serious? You punched me in the face?"

"How did that dumb-ass rookie cop figure out where you were?" Lou yelled at Ken.

"How should I know? Maybe you underestimated his ability."

"No, I didn't. I put him on the case because he has that cowboy attitude. Guns ablazing, taking out the first person he suspected. His grandpa and Juice were the brains of this operation." Lou looked down and saw the limp body of Nolan. Lou walked over to him and kicked Nolan in the ribs.

"Grab him."

Ken grabbed Nolan under his armpits. He fumbled and dropped his body trying to drag Nolan. Ken was making more noise than a bull in a china shop, so Lou grabbed Nolan's legs, and Ken grabbed his shoulders. They took him to Lou's car and placed him in the trunk.

"Take him to the school," Lou said.

"You want me to take an unconscious cop to the school? What the hell am I going to do with him there?"

"You're going to tie him up in Principal Bitton's office."

"Why?" Ken asked.

"So we don't take the fall for killing him. Bitton asked me to take Cory and Juice out of his school. I have the calls recorded still. That fat slob owes me for coming up short on last month's quota."

Ken jolted his head up. "Principal Bitton sells for you? Who the hell in this city don't you have on payroll?"

"Bitton doesn't sell for me! He does keep my books, and I noticed some skimming off the top from my monthly quotas. That's why we need to frame him, find his records, and destroy them."

"Sounds like a plan. I'll have him waiting for you. What are you going to do?" Ken asked.

"I'll be there in a minute. I just need to tie up one more loose end."

Lou grabbed his phone and called Jared. The phone rang a few times and Jared picked up the other end.

"Hello?"

"Jared, what are you doing?"

"I'm heading up to Fillmore like you said. I'm so proud of Nolan for his work in this case."

"Yeah, he really surprised me as well. I still think he should've made the arrest on Cory, but he kept digging, and now he could be on the verge of blowing up."

"I know. Well I've got a long drive ahead. I'll see you up there," Jared said.

"Actually, I got held up here, but we'll talk soon."

"Bummer deal for you. Talk to you soon."

Jared hung up the phone.

# CHAPTER 41

*L*ou strode through the halls slowly and methodically, making his way to the principal's office. The longer he made Nolan wait for his upcoming execution, the better. Lou had learned one thing throughout the years of torturing: the longer the victim waits, the worse they make it for themselves. They practically torture themselves waiting for the actual pain, and that was almost worse than the actual pain. Nolan was going to be extra fun. He'd already experienced what it was like to be a captive. The flashbacks he was going to experience were almost enough for Lou not to do anything else. Almost, but not quite.

Lou stepped in the office and jerked the door shut behind him. Nolan, still dazed, felt his wrists burning. He looked down, and the ropes were tied so tight they were cutting his skin. Lou sat on the desk in front of him. His legs dangled back and forth; his vicious scowl was enough to make Charles Manson tremble.

"Ken said something that got my attention earlier."

Nolan recalled last time he was in this situation that the man doing the torture really didn't want to hear his sufferer say anything; he wanted, more or less, to hear himself talk. Nolan wasn't going to let Lou have any more control over him than absolutely necessary.

"Oh yeah, what did he have to say there, Louis?"

"Did you call me Louis? Nobody has called me that since my mom. She was the only person I allowed to call me that."

"Well Louis, the way I figure it, you don't deserve to be called Lou anymore. Lou is a respected name of a cop who put his life on the line. But I guess you had us all fooled. You're a Louis. That's a name of a coward who continued to put the lives of all his men in jeopardy. Whenever you sent one of us out on a drug bust, you knew that you would kill them if they ever found out the truth behind it."

"Nolan, I'm going to tell you your biggest problem. And you'll be able to trust me on this because I don't give a shit about you, so you'll know there's no sugarcoating it. You're not nearly as smart as you think you are. Reflect back on the last six months of your life. You've been caught and tortured twice. Most cops aren't held captive once in their entire career, and you've managed to do it two different times. You made one of your suspects an informant. I wouldn't have had to pull the trigger on him if you would've arrested him and Cory."

Nolan's blood boiled inside of him. "So it wasn't Ken. At least you have the guts to pull the trigger yourself and not make one of your pigeons do it."

"If you have to question whether I have the guts or not to do my own dirty work, then you are dumber than even I thought. I've pulled the trigger on more men and women then you can count. Of course, I am accounting for how stupid you are and assume you can only use your toes and fingers to count."

"That's a good one. You keep calling me stupid, but it seems to me that I'm the only one who has figured out who the true druglord of St. George is, so maybe you're the stupid one. If I'm as dumb as you say I am, then surely you have to be foolish to be figured out by a simpleton like me."

Lou hopped down off the desk and started searching through the desk drawers. He opened them up and threw the papers all over the room. Nolan beamed, "What's the matter Louis? Trying to change your grade?"

Lou snapped his head around. "I'm looking for the records that I had my good friend Lawrence keep for me all these years. When I first started my business, I wasn't so good with the numbers. I got my college roommate, the math major, to run my numbers. Eventually it evolved into him keeping detailed records on everyone I had to deal with. That includes all the people I've had to take out."

Nolan smirked. "Why, Louis, why would I want to see something like that?"

"You think you have me flustered, but you don't. So you need to shut your damn trap and save some of that oxygen of yours."

"The simple fact that you have to say that means I'm getting inside of your head. It's a dome party, and

I'm the only guest." Nolan raised his eyebrows twice at Lou.

Lou stopped searching, grabbed the chair Nolan was tied to, and rolled it to the center of the room. He squatted down so he was face-to-face with Nolan. "When I find the ledgers, I'm going to show you that you're not the first person to figure out who I was. In fact there have been a couple of people, one in particular I want you to see, but I also want it to shrink that big ego of yours. You may have found out who I am; however, if it wasn't for your grandpa, you would've snagged Cory and Juice, and I wouldn't have had to kill you. Like I said, you're not as smart as you think you are. Until you realize that, you're always going to come up short. Not that it matters anymore."

"Do you really think that Lawrence Bitton was shortsighted enough to hide his criminal activities in his desk at work? He's a math major. Those guys are geniuses, not to mention he's up to date on all the current technology. So unless you took an IT course in the last fifteen minutes, you're never going to find his records."

Lou burst out the door. Nolan wiggled and twisted his hands and wrists, trying to free himself of his binds. He yanked so hard he let out a colossal grunt as he pulled up. He tore deeper into his cuts on his wrists. He was close to losing consciousness from the agony he was causing himself. Lou came back into the office dragging Ken by the shirt. He took him to the computer and flung him down into the chair.

"You know computers. Find my records," Lou said.

"Okay, but you realize it's not that simple. They may not even be on this hard drive."

Nolan cackled loudly. "You don't know what the hell you're doing, do you, Louis?"

Lou dove over to Nolan and began punching him repeatedly. He alternated between his left and right fists, pounding Nolan's face. After twenty or so shots, he stopped. "I told you not to call me Louis."

Nolan spit out blood. "I'm sorry, you're right. You did ask me to stop. You even asked politely. I won't call you Louis. I did notice that your employees call you L, but when I first heard that name I thought of the girls name Elle. So if I can't call you Louis, I'm thinking Ellie-girl might be more appropriate.

Lou continued to use Nolan's face as a punching bag. "You need to learn when to shut your damn mouth."

At this point, Nolan couldn't control his laughing; he knew he had gotten under Lou's skin, but he didn't know how far he could take it. "It took you over thirty punches to give me a cut under my eye and a bloody lip. You hit like the old man you really are."

"Keep laughing; you'll see how funny it is when I kick your head off."

"You can't kick my head off; you'll be lucky not to break your hip. In fact, I bet you can't lift your leg higher than my stomach."

"I think your right." Lou spun around and kicked Nolan in the chest. The chair fell over on its back. In between gasping for air and laughing, Nolan continued to try and free himself. At a different angle, he could feel some freedom from the ropes.

Lou picked him up and pushed the chair to the corner. The restraints tightened up again. "Keep your scrawny little butt in the corner. Next word I hear out of you, I'm going to shoot you. Do you understand?"

Nolan didn't respond. Lou screamed at the top of his lungs, "Do you understand me?"

"Do you want me to answer, because you said you were going to shoot me if I say anything?"

"Always the funny guy until the end."

# CHAPTER 42

*K*en typed furiously on Bitton's computer. "Boss, I think I got something."

Lou lumbered over to the computer and looked. The look on his face was somewhere between dumbfounded and baffled. He kicked Ken out of the chair and scrolled up and down the screen.

"It's all here. Even the business we abandoned in the 80s. I knew that he would be of good use on the payroll."

Lou rose to his feet and made his way over to Nolan. Nolan's hands and wrists were grisly and blood-soaked from battling with the too-tight zip ties. Lou grabbed the back of the chair and wheeled him into the front of the computer screen. He pointed toward a file on the computer.

"Bitton made a list of all the people that I have killed over the years. Some in the line of duty, and some because I'm a little demented. Well, at least it's a file of the ones he knows about. There are some that only God and I know about."

Lou clicked on the file marked "Expired." He scrolled to a link named "partner" and clicked it. Up popped a picture of Nolan's mom, tied up and gagged to a chair just like Nolan was.

Tears slid down his cheeks, and he whimpered, "Why do you have a picture of my mom?"

"I think you already know the answer to that. I have another picture of her for my private collection, but that was more provocative. You're mom used to go wild for a man in blue."

Nolan kicked his legs at Lou and tried to free himself with even more vigor than before. "You're a damn liar. My mom would've never let you touch her. You're an old, wrinkly, sack of crap."

"Believe what you want, youngster, but how would I know about her tramp stamp of the sun if I hadn't slept with her?"

Nolan spit at Lou but missed. Lou scrolled further down the screen. There was another picture of his mom, but this time it was with two bullets in her. Seeing his mom laying there in that graphic image, Nolan finally lost it and began sobbing.

"Oh shut up, you little puke. You're giving me a headache."

Nolan tried to use his shoulders to wipe away his tears. "Answer me one question. It's the least you could do since I get the feeling that you're going to assassinate me."

"You want to know why."

"Yeah. Why on earth would you kill such a beautiful, sweet, loving person like my mom? Cory I can understand. That kid had nothing going for him and was going to end up in prison anyways, but my mom? She did good things in this world."

"I'd be more than happy to clear a couple of things up for you. First, the irrelevant Cory actually was killed by a drug deal gone wrong. Some tweeker who was looking for more than he could afford to buy pulled the trigger and—poof!—Cory's dead. I felt sorry for him, but that's the life he chose to lead. I really didn't have anything to do with that, but I did have something to do with the retaliation."

"What does that mean?" Nolan asked.

"I'm glad you asked. I actually have you to thank for it. Right after I killed Juice, I got on the phone with his uncle Rob. Rob and I go way back, and he always said he would never purchase my merchandise for re-sell. Come to find out, thanks to you selling it to him for so cheap tonight, he's been buying cheap from Juice and making a profit on my drugs for years. So I gave him the option: he could take care of this kid who killed Cory, or I could introduce him to my friend the Grimm Reaper. It didn't take much convincing for him to see things my way."

Nolan dropped his head. "So you know who killed Cory?"

"Sure, I figured that out the next day. I've been a cop for a long time. All the evidence and DNA was there. I needed to find a way to shut this kid up, and thanks to you, I have Rob on the payroll now."

"So Cory's case will go unsolved just like my mom's?"

"You're starting to catch on. It's too bad you couldn't have arrested Cory or Ken. You would still be alive, and you'd never have to find out the gory details of your mom's death."

"You still haven't given me the details. Why did you kill my mother?"

"Are you sure you want to hear this? I could put a bullet in you, and you could ask her yourself if you believe in that kind of stuff."

Nolan wailed at the top of his lungs, "Tell me!"

"Okay, you don't have to be so touchy. I didn't plan on killing your mom the day I did it. I liked her. She kept to herself, did her job, and was easy on the eyes. We did good police work together. She wasn't by the book like your Grandpa Jared was. When we were bored, we would set up speed traps. Man, we used to get so many speeding violations down Combe Road. People already sped on that road, but when we parked at the top and the bottom, we used to get thirty to forty violations a day. She would even bend the rules on how she treated criminals. I watched her once mule-kick some guy that we arrested square in the junk. Rumor has it that dude coughed up blood for a week after the kick. It was just another day at work.

Your grandpa assigned us the streets we needed to patrol that day. I wanted to go solo, but old Jared wanted the two of us to go together for some reason. I thought it was that he suspected that I was the elusive "L" drug dealer, but reflecting on the day's events for many years now, I now realize he was worried about your mom and not me. In some sort of way, I guess you could say Grandpa Jared was responsible for her death as much as I was.

I digress. Let me skip to the good part. For the most part, the story that I told your grandpa is true. We found some punk robbing a local gas station. I recognized him as James right away. He was one of my earliest employees. Your mom shot after him like a bullet coming out of a rifle. I was impressed with how fast she was. In all my years working with her, I'd never seen her move that fast. I hung back. I thought James could outrun her. I mean, he was a pretty fast guy. To my surprise, your mom tackled him about a block away from the store. They fought for a minute, and to my shock, your mom kicked his ass. By the time I got over there, James was in handcuffs, and your mom was standing over him kicking him in the ribs. I loved that about her; she didn't take any shit from anyone.

When she grabbed him and got him to his feet, that idiot, James, started asking for my help. He said things like, you need to help me or I'm going to tell the whole world about your drug deals. I tried to tell him to shut up, but the damage had already been done. I'll never forget her eyes when she realized that I was the one who provided the streets of St. George with drugs. Those eyes haunted me for years. Some nights I still see them, like when a kid realizes their dad is really Santa Clause; she was broken. Everything that I told her and showed her was a lie, and lucky for me, it made her pause long enough to where I could suckerpunch her in the temple and knock her out cold. I unlocked the cuffs off of James and told him to run. A few days later, when he came to pick up his shipment, I stabbed him a few times. I couldn't have him out there robbing any more stores and fingering me as the guy who supplied him.

Let's get back to your mom. So I took her back to my house, and I didn't know what I was going to do with her. She wasn't my first kill, but I could justify killing everyone that I had up to that point. Whether they were some small-time criminal or a drug user, I figured I was doing the world a favor. But your mom, like you said, was a good-hearted being. I couldn't convince myself of any reason she should die."

"Alright stop," Nolan said. "I don't want to hear the rest of it."

"That's too bad because I'm telling you."

"Why? Just shoot me and be done with it."

"No, I've been trying to get under your skin all day. Physical pain wasn't working, and psychological warfare had no effect on you. Now that I've finally found out what works, you want me to stop? I don't think so. Let's get back to the story. This is where it gets good. I had a choice to make. I could let her go, get arrested, serve my time, and maybe get out and work construction the rest of my life. That was best-case scenario. On the other hand, I could kill someone I respected and live my life as a free man. Believe it or not, it wasn't as easy of a decision as you might think it would have been. I went back and forth on what to do, but ultimately, I decided she needed to go. Just to put your mind at ease, you called my bluff. I was never with your mom, but I did sneak a peek when I had her bound."

Nolan writhed in pain, and he had one final attempt to break free, but the pain from the cuts on his wrists put an end to his feeble attempt. He glanced at Lou, and in a deep sadistic voice he'd never heard come out of his mouth he said, "You're sick. It's a shame that a monster like you gets to keep living while an angel like my mom is gone. But I have a feeling you're going to get yours before your life comes to an end. I don't know how or why, but karma is going to get you."

"I've been doing this for a long time, kid. If it was coming for me, it would've already gotten me. Let me finish my story. I made the decision to kill her, but I didn't want to torture her. She was a friend, and I wanted to make it quick. So I put the gun to her back and pulled the trigger. Bang, and just like that, she was gone. The loudness of a gun in a closed room is something you never get used to. It rings in your ears for hours, sometimes even days later I can still hear it. Have you ever heard that ringing, Nolan?"

Nolan shook his head. "No. I've never executed anyone in cold blood."

"Well then this will be a new experience for you." Lou grabbed his Smith and Wesson and shot Ken in the head. Ken's body fell limp, and he twitched a few times. His blood was sprayed all over the wall and carpet. Lou was dead-on about one thing; the ringing in Nolan's ears was unbearable.

# CHAPTER 43

*L*ou gradually wandered over to Ken's inert body. He kicked him lightly with his boots a few times to the stomach.

"He's gone to meet his maker. It's too bad; I respected Ken. He was one of the good ones I dealt with."

Nolan stood up, with the chair still tied to his wrists, and made a break for the door. Nolan's legs churned as fast as he could move them. He got to the door, lowered his shoulder, and rammed through it. The wood holding the deadbolt ruptured, and the door launched open. He searched for the exit. He spotted the south exit that ran right into the teachers' parking lot. He darted for the doors when he felt a burning going up his calf. He tumbled to the ground. He and the chair flipped like a car down the highway that just got sideswiped. The pain in his calf worsened. He felt a warm liquid dribbling up his leg and onto his face. He didn't need to look down to know what happened. Lou shot him. He succumbed to the pain and rested his head on the school's dust-filled carpet.

He sensed Lou standing above him. His felt his chair snatched back in the upright position. Lou got down on one knee. "Why did you run? Where were you going? You've got a chair strapped to you."

"Lou, you've known me for over fifteen years. Did you really think I was going to sit back and let you kill me?" Nolan mumbled the words out. The pain in his calf paralyzed him.

Lou put his gun back in his holster and rolled Nolan back into Bitton's office. "I'm going to spill your blood in here. Not that there's anything special about this office. I don't want to have to clean up more than one room though. Your little escape plan got blood trickled all along the hallway. That is going to cost me an extra grand."

"If you wouldn't have shot Ken, I wouldn't have run. So you can take your extra money and shove it."

"You finally understand how criminals think. That's precisely how I would've put a spin on that situation. It's too bad I'm going to have to kill you. We could've gone far. But you know way too much."

"Is that why you dropped Ken? He knew too much?"

"Yes! Ken has been with me for a few of my slayings. Hell, I would've trusted my life with Ken. He was a wrong-time-wrong-place casualty."

"What does that mean? If you wanted to kill him, you would've done it right after he found the files."

Lou pulled up a chair in front of Nolan. "I was fifty-fifty on whether I was going to do it. I didn't know if I was going to confess to your mom's murder to you. If I would've taken him out right after he found the files, and I didn't inform you of the murder of your mom, that would've made me a real bastard."

Nolan pulled his head back and swung it fiercely at Lou. He smacked Lou on the bridge of the nose. Blood streamed out of the base of the nose. Lou grabbed his nose with his hands and cupped the blood flowing out. He took the butt of his revolver and smacked Nolan across the face.

"Enough play time. Do you want to know why I killed Ken? It's because nobody who knows the truth about your mom gets to live. He understood that I was an assassin, but no one gets to roam the earth knowing I'm a cop killer. I have too much respect for the uniform."

"You have got to be the most deluded person ever. You say you have too much respect for the uniform, but you still go out and execute us?"

"I've only killed one cop. I'm not going to count you because you're not truly one of us. You're a pampered sissy who only got a job because your grandpa pleaded with me."

Lou put his gun to Nolan's temple. "Goodbye Nolan."

Nolan closed his eyes and gripped the armrest as tight as he could. He wondered if he would hear the ringing in his ears after he was dead.

"Open your eyes. I love the look in someone's eyes when they realize they're going to die."

Nolan opened his eyes and smiled. "It's too bad you're not going to get to see that in my eyes then."

"What?" Lou asked.

Nolan gestured with his head for Lou to look behind him. Lou swung his head around and got flattened with a right cross to the jaw. He stared into the eyes of Jared. He went for his gun, but Jared kicked it out of reach.

Jared took his size thirteen, steel-toed boots and punted Lou's face. Lou tried to stand up, but Jared stomped his knee. Nolan heard a blood-curdling scream come out of Lou. Lou's knee went one way, and the rest of his leg the other way. Jared grabbed a pair of handcuffs out of his pants pocket and cuffed one end to Lou and the other end to the leg of the desk.

He rushed over to Nolan and cut the zip ties off him with his pocketknife. Lou was still groggy, trying to regain focus. Jared went and put his boot directly on the broken knee and gave one more crushing stomp to it.

"You were my best friend, Lou. How could you do this to me?"

Jared waited patiently for Lou to answer. "I'm not going anywhere until you tell me."

Lou moaned, "Geez, Jared, you broke my leg. You think you could wait a few seconds for me to deal with the pain before answering you."

Nolan stood up and staggered over to them. He fell down exhausted, right next to Lou. Jared offered his hand to help him up. Nolan waved it off and mustered up enough strength to sit up. He looked over at Lou and beamed.

"Wipe that smirk of your face. You didn't beat me. You had to have Grandpa bail you out one more time. You'll never be anything."

Nolan grabbed one of the speakers from the computer and smashed Lou over the head. "I wouldn't have it any other way than my grandpa saving me."

Nolan slogged over to Jared and embraced him in a bear hug. Jared grasped him back and smiled.

"That's touching. An old man and his dog, but can you arrest me so I can get this leg checked out?" Lou asked.

"Alright."

Jared went over to un-cuff him when Nolan stepped in front of him, "He killed mom. All the files are right there. He's not just a drug dealer, he's L. He's the guy you've been after for years."

Jared sat and gazed at all the crimes Bitton recorded for Lou. "This is unbelievable; you may be the Prince of Darkness himself. You have a file and pictures of all the people that you've murdered? What do you do with the pictures, make a scrapbook?"

"You wouldn't understand, Jared. They're not trophies, but they are sort of like a souvenir."

"So that story you told me about my daughter's murder?"

"I'm not going to retell that twice in one day. If you want to know, ask him, or come find me in a few months in prison."

"But you told me you tracked down every lead on her death. You even sent me on a few."

"I lied. What did you think I was going to do? Oh, by the way, boss, I killed your daughter; you better lock me up. I was lucky you were the chief when I killed her. Any other person would've dug deeper into one of their own being killed, but between your emotional distress and trust of me, I got away with murdering a fellow cop and your daughter."

"That's enough," Nolan said. "I'm taking you to the station and booking your ass. Don't worry, I'll make sure to come and visit you until you're dead. That shouldn't be long, seeing as you've put a lot of people in the Point of the Mountain prison over the years.

Nolan un-cuffed him from the desk and cuffed him with his hands behind his back.

"Take the handcuffs off, son," Jared said.

"What? No way, Grandpa, he's going to pay for what he did."

"Yes he is, Nolan. Yes he is."

Nolan took the restraints off of Lou and went and stood behind Jared.

"What are you going to do, Jared? You've always gone by the book. In fact, we used to laugh at you behind your back and call you Mother Teresa because you always tried to look at the best in everyone, even the deplorable criminals you arrested. You always gave them some sort of pep talk after you busted them to make them feel better."

"None of them ever killed my only child and tried to kill my grandson."

"So this is how it's going to end with us? I don't think you have it in you. So why don't you put that gun down, and we can settle this like men. Besides, I have no doubt that Nolan is going to jump in once I get the best of you, and trust me, I'm going to get the best of you even with one leg."

Jared tossed his gun to Nolan. "Don't jump in no matter what. Do you understand, Nolan?"

316

"Yes, sir. You've got this, Grandpa."

Lou hobbled over and threw a punch. Jared easily ducked it and stuck his pocketknife into the ribs of Lou as he came up. He pulled the knife out, and Lou toppled.

He clutched the wound and applied pressure to get it to stop bleeding. Jared stood over Lou like a giant. Lou pleaded, "Alright, old friend, arrest me. I'll go quietly. I'll admit to everything I've done, I'll give you Bitton, I'll give all the credit to Nolan for breaking the case. He'll be on the fast track to anywhere he wants to go. Taking down the corrupt police chief, he'll be able to punch his own ticket to youngest lead detective in SGPD history. Please don't kill me."

"Did my little girl beg for her life?"

"No, she didn't. She was a rock, just like you raised her. You would've been so proud. She didn't even cry."

"Would you have shown mercy if she did?"

"Of course I would've; you know me, Jared. You can't kill me. That makes you no better than I am."

"You're right, I do know you. I know when you're lying. You didn't show her any mercy, and I'm not going to show you any."

Jared took his knife and stabbed him in the throat. Lou gasped and wheezed for oxygen. He floundered throughout the office and finally fell. He died with his hands clutched around his neck.

Nolan grabbed a chair and collapsed into it. "So that's that, huh?"

"I guess so."

"How did you find me, Grandpa? I told you to meet at Lou's house."

"I was a cop for a long time. I deducted that this was the only place you could've ended up."

"How did you do that?"

"I had someone track your cell phone."

Nolan bowed his head to Jared. "Yeah, Lou may have been a mastermind criminal, but he never could catch up to modern technology. I'm just glad you were able to."

Jared asked with a somber voice, "Where's Juice?"

"He's gone."

"Who did it, Ken or Lou?"

"Ken and Lou both claimed Lou did it, but I think it was Ken. I was there, and I didn't see Lou anywhere. I even explored the entire alley just like you taught me. I kept Ken engaged with our conversation while I moved around, checking to see if anyone else was there."

"Do you want me to tell his parents?" Jared asked.

"No, I'll tell them. I want to tell them about his Uncle Rob getting him into the life. Those two have enough influence to get him investigated.

"Good thinking, Nolan. The only thing I'm trying to wrap my mind around is I get why Ken would blame Lou, but why would Lou say he did it if Ken killed Juice?"

"I don't know, maybe to build his lore? I don't really know if Ken did it. I don't really care. I'm going to call this in and get an ambulance over here. I have a bullet in my leg."

"Yeah, we better get that checked out."

# CHAPTER 44

Nolan pulled into Karen's house before he went home for the evening. Karen ran out and jumped into the passenger side of the car. Nolan caught a glimpse of Coach Porter staring out the front window. Nolan stuck his hand out the window and gave him a wave. Coach Porter waved back and shut the drapes.

"You two seem to be getting along better," Karen said.

"Baby steps. Just when he realizes I'm not a disrespectful little goon, I start dating his daughter. It's every dad's job to have animosity toward their teenage daughter's boyfriend."

"Especially when he's an old man."

"Wow, low blow. Since when is a twenty-three-year-old considered an old man?"

Karen brushed her hair behind her ear. "When he claimed to be an eighteen-year-old high school senior."

Nolan's face flushed beet red. "I had to; it was my job."

Karen snickered. "It's okay; I don't want to date anyone other than my old man. I can't handle dating high school boys anymore; too much drama, unlike you who never has anything dramatic going on in his life."

"Do I detect a little sarcasm?"

"You're the detective; you tell me."

Nolan opened the driver-side door and stretched his calf out the door.

"How's the rehab coming?"

"Slow, but I'm gaining my strength back. Not like when I lifted with Juice, but I'm starting to feel like I'm close to one hundred percent."

Karen peered out the window. "Have you talked to his parents lately?"

"Not since his funeral. They're still grieving, from what I've heard. My grandpa talked to them a few weeks back, and they're still pretty upset with us. I don't blame them. If I wouldn't have made him my informant, he would still be alive."

"He would've been in prison though," Karen said.

"That's true, but he would've been out in a couple of years."

"We're doing a special tribute to Juice and Cory at graduation. Christy is actually going to mention Cory in her valedictorian speech."

"That's nice. Who's going to be overseeing graduation?"

"What do you mean?"

"I arrested Principal Lawrence Bitton. I highly doubt that he's going to give out the diplomas."

"One of the vice principals; I don't really have any idea. Something has been bothering me for some time,

Nolan, and I'm optimistic that you can answer it."

"What's that?"

"Why did Lou and Principal Bitton bring you into the school if they were the leaders of the drug ring they assigned you to catch?"

"I have sat and pondered that question myself for a long time. I'm not sure I have the exact answer, but I'm certain it's one of two reasons. First, they wanted Cory and Juice arrested. When Lou had me tied up, he kept saying if I would've arrested Cory this wouldn't be happening. He assigned me because he didn't have the foreknowledge that I would keep digging. He thought I would make the easy bust and move on to the next case."

"That's logical," Karen said. "What's the second reason?"

Nolan pulled his leg back into the car and shut the car door, and his voice got low-pitched. "The second reason gives me chills up and down my spine because I think it's the real reason he sent me in. I think he sent me in because he thought I was going to fail. He didn't have any faith in me after I botched my previous assignment. I think he thought I wouldn't be able to figure anything out. I don't know what I would've done without the help of Juice and my grandpa. When Lou tortured me, none of the physical pain bothered me as much as his psychological mind tricks he did. He told me that my grandpa had to get me a job. Lou wasn't going to hire me. I wasn't good enough to make the cut."

Karen snatched Nolan's hand and caressed it. "What does that son of a bitch know? He's been murdering, torturing, and growing drugs since the 80s. If he didn't think you were a good enough cop, then I would consider that a compliment. The fact that he put you there proves that he's the dumb cop, not you."

Nolan's face brightened up. "Maybe you're right. I was a bad cop before, but now that my grandpa is the interim police chief, I've been a sponge—soaking up as much information and knowledge as he'll teach me."

"How does old Jared like the new job?'

"If he hears you call him old, he'll challenge you to a race."

Karen laughed. "I'm sure he would. Can I ask you something really personal?"

"Sure, I'm an open book."

"What really happened between Lou and your grandpa that night?"

"What do you mean?"

"How did Lou really die?"

"The news report is accurate. My grandpa burst through the door and saw Lou's gun to my head. He and my grandpa wrestled around for a little bit. He had my grandpa pinned down when my grandpa slid his pocketknife out and stabbed him in the ribs. He reached for his gun, and my grandpa slit his throat out of desperation."

"Okay, I guess." Karen shrugged her shoulders.

"That's the way the evidence points. Charges were never brought up; hell, the district attorney asked him to fill in as chief."

Karen leaned over and kissed Nolan on the cheek. "I wouldn't have cared if he shot him in the back of the head in cold blood. Lou was Satan himself, and our town is safer now that he's off the streets and not in charge of our police force."

"For now, but some other thug is going to see an opportunity to sling drugs."

"Yeah, and you'll be there to bust him."

www.ingramcontent.com/pod-product-compliance
Lightning Source LLC
LaVergne TN
LVHW052014080426
835513LV00018B/2027